DEAR GOD, DEAR DR. HEARTBREAK
NEW AND SELECTED POEMS

Dear God, Dear Dr. Heartbreak
New and Selected Poems

by

Aliki Barnstone

The Sheep Meadow Press
Riverdale-on-Hudson, NY

Designed and typeset by The Sheep Meadow Press
Distributed by The University Press of New England

All inquiries and permission requests should be addressed to the publisher:

The Sheep Meadow Press
PO Box 1345
Riverdale, NY 10471

Library of Congress Cataloging-in-Publication Data

Barnstone, Aliki.
  Dear God, dear Dr. Heartbreak : new and selected poems. poems / by Aliki Barnstone.
      p. cm.
  I. Title.
  PS3552.A72D43 2009
  811'.54--dc22
                                    2009038293

Acknowledgments

Grateful acknowledgment is made to the journals in which the following poems have appeared, often in different form.

From *Madly in Love:*
    American Literary Review: "The Suicides," "Dream of Orchids," "The Bath," "Bright Snow," *Berkeley Poetry Review:* "Imperative."

From *Wild With It:*
    Barrow Street: "You Will," *Boulevard:* "Months in the Frozen World," *The Drunken Boat* (www.thedrunkenboat.com): "Wild With It," "Wild Wind," "Blue," "Bathing Jesus," *Faultline:* "Wild Wind," *Manoa:* "Blue," *New Letters:* "The Train to the Millennium," "With Walt Whitman on the Staten Island Ferry," "Wavelength Revelation," *Ploughshares:* "You Open Your Hands," *The Southern Review:* "Inevitable Move," "The June my Greek Grandmother Lay Dying in a Queen's Hospital," *Southwest Review:* "Purple Crocuses." "Blue" and "Bathing Jesus" appear in *Voices of Light: Spiritual and Visionary Poems by Women Around the World from Ancient Sumeria to Now* (Shambhala Publications, 2000), edited by Aliki Barnstone. "Bathing Jesus" appears in *Archetypes of the Collective Unconscious: Reflecting American Culture Through Literature and Art,* edited by Mark Waldman (Tarcher / Putnam).

From *Blue Earth:*
    Agni: "A Declining Neighborhood," *Antioch Review:* "On the Hottest San Francisco Day in Recorded History He Plays Piano and She Listens," *Artful Dodge:* "Blue Room, Blue Horse," *Berkeley Poetry Review:* "Sensual Pleasure That Is Achieved Morbidly, Corruptingly," *Chicago Review:* "Spirals," *Crab Orchard Review:* "Seen from my Window in San Francisco," *Exquisite Corpse (www.corpse.org):* "More than a Month of Gray Winter in Madison," "The Ferry to Serifos," "Go to the Good and Return with the Good," *The Graham House Review:* "Brothers," *The Malahat Review:* "Blue Earth," "Counting Time on Kímolos," *New England Review:* "Sadness," *New Letters:* "A Night in Rome," *Partisan Review:* "The Irises of the Midwest," *Prairie Schooner:* "Street Names," "Greek Easter," *TriQuarterly:* "Dream with Billie Holiday," *Witness:* "The Black Room." "Winter and War on Lake Monona" appeared in *A Glass of Green Tea—With Honig,* edited by Susan Brown, Thomas Epstein, & Henry Gould. (Providence, RI: Apephoe Books, 1994).

From "New Poems":

Smartish Pace: "The Crazy Ghost Loses the Use of Her Right Arm,"
"The Crazy Ghost Hears the Music," *The Drunken Boat (www.thedrunkenboat.com/
evapoems.html):*
"The Blue House," "The Destruction of the Jewish Graveyard, Thessaloniki, 1942,"
"The Yellow House in Thessaloniki, 1943," "Day Breaks on Andros, 1944," "Island
Elegy," "Red Picnic, 1946," "1949," *Tikkun:* "A Chat with God about This and
That."

I am grateful for a grant from the Pennsylvania State Council on the Arts that
helped me complete *Wild With It.* I received a senior scholar fellowship from the
Fulbright Foundation and a sabbatical from the University of Nevada, Las Vegas to
write the poems in "Eva's Voice," during which time I lived in Greece for nineteen
months and I also composed all of the poems in "Pique: A Verse Drama."

My gratitude also extends to the artists that produced several of these poems as
collaborations with other media. Frank Haney accompanied me on guitar and
piano on our CD, *Wild Wind.* Robert Barnstone made several of the poems in this
book part of his sculptural installation, "The Narrative Forest."

For the years of help, it is impossible to express enough gratitude to my family,
friends, teachers, and editors, or to name them all, I am so abundantly blessed. Yet
I must acknowledge Willis Barnstone and Alan Michael Parker, who read virtually
every poem in this volume, often at their initial composition. Their transformative
comments have made me a better poet.

Michael S. Harper, my professor at Brown University, made me see a new earth
by directing me to read marvelous poets, most (but not all) of whom were African
–American and at that time (1976) were not canonized. He gave me a life long
mission, both as a translator and an editor, to bring largely unheard voices to the
academy and to print. He set ablaze my love of jazz one late night when I heard
him read from *Dear John, Dear Coltrane* accompanied by a sax. Michael once told
Anthony Walton, "Boy, I'm gonna teach you things you ain't gonna understand
for 10 or 20 years." I guess it took me over 30. I hope that the title of this book in
some measure acknowledges and honors Michael's influence.

OTHER BOOKS BY ALIKI BARNSTONE

POETRY
The Real Tin Flower
Windows in Providence
Madly in Love
Wild With It
Blue Earth

TRANSLATION
The Collected Poems of C.P. Cavafy: A New Translation

LITERARY CRITICISM
Changing Rapture: Emily Dickinson's Poetic Development

ANTHOLOGIES
A Book of Women Poets from Antiquity to Now
with Willis Barnstone

The Calvinist Roots of the Modern Era
with Michael Manson & Carol J. Singley

The Shambhala Anthology of Women's Spiritual Poetry (paperback edition of *Voices of Light: Spiritual and Visionary Poems by Women Around the World from Ancient Sumeria to Now*)

EDITION
Trilogy by H.D.
Introduction and Readers' Notes by Aliki Barnstone

For Craig and Zoë

There is no fear in love; but perfect love casts out fear. I John 4:18

TABLE OF CONTENTS

FROM MADLY IN LOVE (1997)

MADLY IN LOVE

For Ruth Stone

Late one summer night he tore through
her latched screen door, his trousers
in his hand, and declared his love.
Then he lay down on the rug and screamed.
He was obliging when she asked him to leave
and hiked from Goshen twenty miles
across the Brandon Gap in his underwear.
At six AM, casually as if he carried
a sack of breakfast bagels, he rang
our bell, trousers still in hand.
Three days later he committed himself.
He was a librarian, a sensible man.

As a child it mystified me.
Now I think despair could make me
walk twenty miles in my underwear.
I could lie down half-naked and wail
for an audience for my articulate loins.
I've screamed--haven't you?--even though
screaming means no one will listen.
And he was a librarian--I imagine him
knowing all the proper places for books
and for the lover in the stacks
who wasn't there when he clicked off
the fluorescent lights and drove

into mountains where the Milky Way's
silk sash billowed above him
and crickets sang out crazy excitement
as he stood on the dirt road with mountains
rising over him, wonderful, dark,
breathing desire. He saw her lighted
by a lamp and the fire, reading.
And for a moment, before he broke
through the obstructing screen,
liberating to the inside
mosquitoes and winking fireflies,
he thought she might respond.

HIS DESIGN

After the funeral we swam in the pool
of the beautiful apartment building
my uncle--he who chose to end it--designed.

Every entrance was different, nothing
was identical and nothing could erase identity.
The copper edge-banding bled intentionally

into soft stucco, so fleshy and warm
against the bright Texas sky--and all reflected
in abundant windows and in the inviting pool,

the graceful, double-bellied pool,
Mexican-tiled, where we floated
or on whose edges we sat dangling

our feet into the water, parents and children,
aunts and uncles, nieces and nephews,
cousins and siblings, assuming our places

in the design that was not a design
but the accident of birth and of that unaccidental
death which assumed its place, too, and looked out

of the waters of this perfectly placed, perfectly
shaped pool where we laugh, search, talk,
or tell the story again of *why, how, if,*

and, *but no it couldn't be helped*
He was so sick but charming and a genius
and we loved him.

And again tell the story of what
came before and how inscrutably
we arrived at today,

each culpable, each susceptible,
now part of the design,
gathered here in his beautiful pool.

A BEAUTIFUL DAY

Let me stand here. And let me pretend I see all this. . .

C.P. Cavafy

Transient clouds sail in clarity, the trace of moon floats suspended
    between day and night, and I wish I could suspend time, stop here

and look longer than I can at so much loveliness, perfect light
    moving quickly, varying these myriad colors, contrary light moving

fast yet in slow-motion caresses. Let me pretend I can see all this without blurring
    the beauty with loss, that I am saved mid-fall—as if by parachute—and drift

with the wind chimes and all at once—so much singing!—when sparrows,
    finches, chickadees, robins, blue jays, fluting cardinals flicker from tree to tree,

bird-multitudes, wings beating out their wild time and mine, too.
    Let me practice idiot glee—nothing is still!—and I could hold in me

this beautiful changing and changing day through any misery.

THE SUICIDES

Even if I tell you the details of the funeral, the sentiments
of the eulogies, the moment I cried, that three white calla lilies

lolled their heads on the casket lid, that I let some earth fall
from my hand, then stood after the service with my family,

watching from a distance as a bulldozer finished the work
and filled in the grave, you must know our truth--

the suicides are never buried. The undead, they walk the face
of the earth not thanks to their uneasy souls but to make us

uneasy. My uncle slips into the passenger seat of my car,
recounting stories about us, planning a family event, analyzing

a design, telling a joke. I'm driving a Buick special, built
the year of my birth, laughing at his cleverness, glancing

into my rearview mirror, which catches my grandfather, dapper
in a gray flannel suit and a fedora, grinning at my cheek,

proving his repute as a magician-salesman—he thumps his head
and jostles diamonds from his ear and from his sleeve

gold Swiss watches drop into his palm and from his coat pocket
arise Mexican silver goblets, wine-filled. His words are hummingbirds

darting about in the boxed air of the car--he's talking manic expansion
to my uncle—business is booming—they're so glad I'm going their way,

they say, calling out directions, *left!* and *right!* at once, and won't I go
straight into air at the hairpin curve—drop to dream—

into my red-blanketed bed—the darkened room—snow-lighted windows
where my insomniac eyes blink at winter trees, those iced-over gashes

on the night's skin. Why must they sit at the foot of my bed,
so intriguing, whispering the family names with love?

What's the secret question? Who's next? Even if I tell you our story
and more, even if you hold me now, if you want me and answer me,

I hear their voices in your kiss breathing, "It's only for a while."
Nights, nights like this when I'm chasing—what?—down a path

where there are no forks, the brambles are thick, dangerous,
closing in behind me, and I can't separate the roses

from the thorns, turn, stop, or go back. Do you see what I see?
Love goes away and tonight I'm invisible—even these words.

FAIRY TALE

Before the good prince takes the good maid away
the fairy casts a spell on the evil sisters.

Each time they speak, lizards and snakes and toads
fall hissing from their mouths, as if the body

held in all bad and all the bad released
embodied. Now since we're undressed for love

and love's a hard word, a lump in our throats,
a woman appears casting spells with her hands.

Her touch is awful, hurts, is good. Something
unspeakable she forces from our bodies.

It's worse than dirty. Not urine or feces
or what we know of sickness and of health.

It must be venom in all consistencies,
the human secretions of anger, turning

toward and away, touch withheld and resentment,
the child happy and fearless, then ashamed.

Afterward you'd think we'd be cleansed. We have
a quiet moment, hope, a kiss. But before

we're good again, I must be like the girl
who knit the sweater out of nettles, then

wore it, who sucked three iron loaves to nothing
while walking barefoot through desert and winter.

I'll live in three houses, and love and lose
each one. I must have three odious husbands:

one who bores me, one who won't let me out
of sight, one who beats me. Then I'll be free

to kiss you again. Then I'll wake from this dream
just as I did this morning. Spring light warmed

the sheets, my skin--so I wanted to love
you in the sun. You would not hear my words

or feel my touch. I saw my evil sisters--
and all around me, hateful slithering things.

WITH SKATERS AND HORSES IN CENTRAL PARK

Someone falls. I'm looking for the artist
        and while a few skate backwards
                to the beat and glide with easy feet, I spot
        no spinning dancer, no beautiful lover of the ice.
The crowd holds hands in groups:
        some skate in a train, some guide a novice friend.
                They look happy—the first Saturday of the New Year,
        they're together, lovers and families. I walk away
over boulders whose crevices shine
        with bottle shards, vestiges of years
                of smashed teenagers whose joy is to destroy,
        past a man, mesmerized, tossing biscuits to seagulls
who dive for their crumbs, then soar
        over the unfrozen pond next Wollman Rink
                where the crowd waits in line
        to skate in circles with the crowd,
back to the street and the line of carriages and horses,
        the smell of horse, a bored driver
                in top hat drinking coffee from a styrofoam cup,
        tourists with blanketed knees, pointing and talking.
The last horse, a white one, waits, head down.
        I hold out my hand for him to smell,
                run my fingers along his enormous jaw and feel
        the sweet, soft fur of his nose.
He lifts his face away from me, then bows his head
        for more. I palm the place between his eyes,
                stroke his muscular neck, and again he sways
        away from me and toward me, as I leave
and turn back to see him slowly shifting from hoof to hoof,
        his head rising and sinking, as if he were mimicking
                my dance of vulnerability, longing, and resistance.

BRIGHT SNOW

Our winter is unimaginable
to those in other geographies.
The dailiness, the duration, the extremes.

First are preparation and work:
the miracle plastics stretched
with a hair-dryer across old, drafty windows,

the bales of hay stacked up
to farmhouse sills,
the corn cut down to stubble--

and gardeners prune
their prized roses hard
and make mounds of mulch

to protect their perennials.
Some bulbs must freeze
to bloom, but too deep a cold

leads other plants to death not rest.
Then come darkness and bitterness,
shrinking days, the solstice.

The melancholy landscape is
everywhere gray and heavy.
How could we humans have come

this far North where the wind
pricks us with a million needles?
No wonder our muscles contract.

No wonder we turn to each other,
each equally helpless when days are dayless.
Then at last, after the New Year,

comes the bright snow.
It snows all day and night
for three days and nights

and one morning we wake up to find
that snow is the sun's
cold but light-filled twin.

It's early.
Though the snow-plow heaved by
and cast yellow spinning lights

a moment on predawn bedroom walls,
the snow is mostly untouched,
and cars—unscraped and undug-out—

rise like a school of white whales
out of the ocean of snow.
Deep bright snow.

This is the illusion of payment:
that despair is a price paid
for the snow-covered field

to become the sun's iridescent twin
and for each broken corn stalk
catching the afternoon sun

like a gold coin—
though that glow is nothing
but decaying stubble.

It's as ordinary as winter and work
and the voice that says,
bright snow.

BETH SAYS SHE'S MOURNING THE PASSING OF WINTER

My friend Beth says she's mourning the passing of winter,
    the months of white desolation
        which are also freedom

and access to expanses
    we can't traverse
        in warmer months

when we stand on the lakeshore
    throwing out fluorescent green tennis balls
        for our dogs to swim after and happily retrieve

while those who own boats
    own the waters.
        But in winter we can all walk on water.

In spite of skiers, skaters, ice-sailers, ice-fishermen
    and their lonely huts,
        the frozen lakes are mostly empty,

and we walk far,
    anywhere we want.
        The snow says,

Shhh. Shhh. Shhh.
    So we listen
        to the enormous quiet.

Yesterday it thawed.
    Today the temperature fell to two below zero
        and with Beth I mourned the passing of winter

because the iced trees
    made a web of light
        in the blue morning.

Mist flooded the air
    above the Yahara River
        as its waters refroze.

I thought of the Chinese Sung landscape painters
    who practiced technique mechanically and painstakingly
        to prepare for the moment

when passion would quickly guide them
    —hand, brush, ink, and
        eye—

to know where to leave
    blank
        so mist can sing its silence

to solid rocky peaks,
    where to draw the smallest stick bridge
        over a chasm

and the smallest meditating human soul crossing
    into whiteness.
        And

I thought the drunken Sung poet-painters
    were like us,
        tiny companions walking together praising

a landscape brutally cold and bright
    that extends beyond our scope
        into thaw and loss

like the thousand frozen trees
    branching into seemingly infinite, fractured
        light.

MARCH WINDS

The snow is gone. Here and there one can spy
patches of ice. More often quiet green
pushes up in the fields where earlier a brief thaw
followed by a freeze glassed the snow

as if countless ponds shone everywhere.
Damp winds blow off the lakes seeping through coats
and I'm impatient, chilled, taunted by odd warmths.
It's easy to be content with the dry zeros

that chap the skin, to be quiet indoors
or walk the frozen lake on a blue day,
watchful in a world contracted in ice,
and sharp, where people slide in angular

light. Now tulips and irises poke green
butterknives through dark dirt. I sense
wisteria over my head, the scent, urgent
kisses, passion and dissatisfaction.

ARGUMENT

I escape out onto the front porch swing.
Through windows of apartments across the street,

I see the inner walls where dramas play
in lightning and flickering, urgent

shifts of scene and coy narrative winks,
the TV programs numb eyes watch. Ubiquitous evil,

I think, then revise (no, just a common seduction)
feeling now what is *now* is

a science fiction society which I imagine
as if I were apart from it.

I kick the porch rail, sail
back toward the house—forward toward the lake.

Of course—I pray—retreat—and rage—grieve.
Gimme a break. If I weren't disoriented—

so damn dizzy—I'd stamp my foot and cry,
Why keep rehearsing this dumb drama?

I don't even want to talk about it.
I jump from the swing, leaving it swinging,

and stomp my feet down stairs to the lake shore
where I spiral inward to *I, I, I,*

outward to the night
and lake coiling under the waning moon,

a fine, wide-spanning bowl tilted in air,
pouring its light into numb waters.

But fuck it. The lake is still dark
with my smart misery.

IMPERATIVE

The men are dead. Yes, and the boys are dead, too.
Let's take them in our arms and weep
because they are cold and unreachable.
Let's kick the dirt gleefully into their graves
because they are cold and unresponsive.
Let's go home and pound the walls
because our beds are empty
and we didn't get what we wanted.
Let's rock numbly in our chairs blaming ourselves
because we chose it
and we got exactly what we wanted.
Let's raise them from the dead,
let's kiss the breath back into them and tease
their penises erect. Let's do it before we die.
Let's fill their minds with glory and possibility
and take them inside us and let them
fill us with glory and possibility.
Let's say, let's do it again.
Let's examine our histories and bury the dead,
resurrect them and kiss them again and again.
Let's hope. Let's take them in our arms and weep.

DREAM OF ORCHIDS

I've watered and fed my marvelous orchids, safeguarded them
        from root-rot, let them drain in the kitchen sink
               before placing them back in the light.
I've protected them from winter drafts with plastic stretched
        to near perfect transparency.
              I've waited
through their dormancy and loved
        their thick, sturdy leaves.
             Their blossoms last for months after months of nothing.
And their petals feel like the smooth skin of sex
        and they smell like the first day the ice breaks
            and the river's rushing is like breath quickening
when love's exposed,
        when neighbors swing dance in the park gazebo
            and kids shoot hoops—the ball sounds
like *poomf! poomf! poomf!*
        like a love drug,
            like a memory freed from the clock
(whose sound we make the smallest plot,
        when we say it says *tick-tock*).
            And when they bloom again, they soar
like rare birds in the house air, which they turn
        to some wildness, a crazed, shifting light of tall trees' foliage—
            so beautiful is everything moving.
My orchids are like orioles drinking orange juice,
        heavenly bluebirds, the wood duck with its red eye shining
            as it drifts backward with the current,
or the great blue heron gliding, while under its gaze
        were the Wisconsin River, sand bars, and mist,
            and me whispering to my dog, "Hold still."

★ ★ ★

I invite a woman and a man into my dream house
        and I show off my orchids. "How lovely!" they exclaim
            and I feel sheltered and warm,

a hothouse flower among hothouse flowers.
 And then woman breaks off the orchids' heads,
  leaving ragged stems strewn on the window sill.
And she pins the orchids to her bosom, as if they'd been cultivated
 to decorate her cheap prom dress—
  and she stands up straight and smiles too big
for the white out of the camera flash.
 And when she turns to the man for admiration,
  and when he takes her in his arms and wants her
to be one with him, and when he croons,
 there are no limits, no walls,
  I see—at last—she is me.

MOON

Who in her right mind talks to the moon? I do.
Tonight I make my request: help me.
And the moon steadily fills the dark with itself,

its face open-mouthed as if, calling out in suffering
long ago, its expression remained fixed and its light
kept changing, as tonight its familiar visage

plays on the water and brightens the summer ripples
moving in a slight breeze and humid heat—
such quickness and such heaviness—white blades

shifting against each other, a fast-handed crowd
sharpening knives, my mind slicing away excess.
Once I prayed to moon: let him who is far away

think of me when he looks in your face, the way lovers do
whose faith is strong. But doubt severs the light-cut lake
(a mirror of the moon's countenance, or maybe mine)

from the whole neighborhood where we used to live.
The houses rendered shadows look deserted and I learn
not to fill them in, not even under the full moon's brief watch.

FOR BUCK

When we leave, Buck chases the car
for miles out of town. Then brought home

again, howls a dirge all night.
Who can say the dogs don't suffer loss?

I think they mourn with absolute purity,
with no words to form a memory, consolation

or hope of return.
Today what we assume confuses me,

the faith that each leave-taking is temporary.
The dog yelps out his happiness

each time he sees us, and now our scents
still linger in the carpet where he lies,

but we're not there—no hands in his fur,
no voices saying his name. And so at night

he urgently goes to each house we took him to,
searching for the ghostly human friends.

ENDING

The rain has stopped and I stand in our yard
in my bare feet though the stones are cold.
The young trees we planted release tiny leaves
in their first spring--the crab apple, the stand of birches,
the two apples, two cherries, two pears, the red maple.

So too have the early spring flowers begun to bloom:
daffodils, tulips, Dutchman's britches, flox,
grape hyacinths, bleeding heart, and bloodroot,
whose flowers, chaste white spheres, close-petaled,
bloom close to the ground and to their red, staining roots.

Perennials are a strange faith--what's nurtured
and loved, protected from cold and disease, endures
as if order were beautiful, redeems our hope
and the measure of joy with which we chose our plants
then waited for the colors they make in their freedom.

Soon this will not be mine. It's dark, what's called
the wee hours--and so they seem too short to me.
The rain drops peep with the night birds and insects
and with the train baying to warn of its own passing
Into silence and nothing, I think. Then correct myself,
since a train goes to the city named a destination—

and it is merely me who hears a short-lived cry extinguished,
and feels mid-western cut limestone, a garden path,
the soles of my feet on cold, wet stones...

SOLSTICE

Dogs howl with the wind, who
knows why. I guess they know what they know—
some of us thrill when stillness deepens
just before the sky turns green and
the streets turn into green rivers,
and alarms and radio
electrify the city
with warnings to take shelter
for out on the plains
tornadoes spin toward our city
and dogs howl out love,
and we howl
with the dogs
and play piano, guitars,
spoons, bongos, kazoos,
slap our thighs red,
and thunder while the storm's
ardent, wet, bright, thrashing,
humid air mixes with sweat and I
dance as if I could stand being
solo another light, summer hour—
and all around me, so many
hands flourishing.

A HUMID SUMMER DAY

How humid it is today, the sparrows darting
in and out of tall trees.
Why can't I love you as I love what we made?

The heaviness of hands, the lightness of hands.

I overlook the garden I shared creating.
Oriental lilies, ferns, cosmos and daisies revel in moisture;
hostas spread wide wings over black earth;
vegetables wait for harvest.

The cardinal's whistle sears the sky.

But heat and wetness, so beneficial to plants,
are restraining hands on my head.
Heavy hands, light hands.

Herbs and roses scent the air.

I love you is a spell cast by poems, TV, radio songs,
by summer and its trance of bounty: long days of light
and sleeplessness,

the spreading verdure of the land,
the sky glazing green before unleashing storm,
tornadoes, rivers flooding their banks,

agitated dreams, desire.

The heaviness of hands, the lightness of hands.

Summer in the earth and in the sky acts out its abundance
while I speak out scarcity:

I'll leave you with the hindsight
of the blankness on the other side of plenty,

vast blank fields of snow--

all the possibilities following this
blank page.

SO THIS IS GRIEF

The day I see the first winter light, the professor
in his worn suede jacket stands in the parking lot
while a few still yellow leaves

blow wearily about. His face is gray like the sky
and the students walk to class, sick of the routine.
So this is grief.

Three hyacinth glasses gleam in the dishrack,
tinged with green, ready for me to fool bulbs into belief
that it's spring.

And the bulbs wintering in the refrigerator
lean their purple skins against the cider.
The way it is with me, words can't help.

Now that we're estranged--strange word--for good,
analysis doesn't matter. How might it feel
to go back again and pass the house

I no longer own where strangers hang their coats
in the vestibule? They'll sink into an easy chair
on a day so cold the keys stick in the doors.

They'll live in the living room, and will they notice
the frozen lake I focused into a hardness of thought,
a moment slicked over like the first day of solid ice?

I could walk as far as I wanted there, feet passing
over the lake's lens amplifying weeds and depths.
It did no good to talk about what we saw.

So this is grief. You have red hair.

THE BATH

I'm taking a bath thirty-six years, seven months,
and three days after my birth.

Outside I hear the city of Madison hum out
its dumb question, *Hu-u-uh?* One long, constant note.

No sirens or screams, no tornado warning, no people
laughing on the street because it's spring, nothing like that.

Inside the bathwater clicks or plinks,
clearing its throat or breathing regularly,

saying *please, please, please, please, please,*
ditto, and ditto again, like that, under its breath,

so you just make out its loneliness. I hear these things
because I'm asking, *Am I inside my body? Am I a work of art?*

and prop myself up, so one calf and ankle and foot,
then the other, float. So one forearm and wrist and hand,

then the other, float. Skin in warm water is rosy.
Breasts float like water lilies.

I am a woman who's not given birth, soaking the tension
out of my back, alone in the bath, seeing if I can

objectify myself while my heart goes out to some you,
out through the fogged window, sighing like the body

of water—warm, elusive—out over the dumb groan of city
and the slushy, melting lakes streaked with those signs

of both solitude and society: lights of streets, windows, cars.
This is not what we call longing, yearning, desire, horniness.

This is not a memory of someone who admired my body
or with touch transported me inside myself.

Can you imagine something else? Not the image of lovers
in the mind of a woman alone in the bath, speaking to the

blankness of bathroom walls or the blankness of the page.
Imagine now I can't see my face, only these floating hands,

heels hooked on the bathtub's rim, these strange, weighted
limbs, unfamiliar a moment, though little changed in years,

as if I were newborn and had no words and no past,
no way to identify this—this what?—this thing lying in water,

trying to unwind, a little bitter to be alone in her body,
questioning, pleading, trying to please, and unable to exit

her conversation with you or the pleasure of these words
forming out of water, the pleasure of being in the bath.

FROM WILD WITH IT (2002)

BLUE

She must have been there
the morning my daughter was born,
blue in the windows;

the narrow glass in the hospital walls
let in her pale spring light.
She hides in the forget-me-nots in the wallpaper,

flutters in the doctors' and nurses' dull medical gowns,
glints in the metal of the scissors that cut the cord.
Her threads embroider the bloody placenta.

She tints the newborns' eyes with her cyan hand,
for babies come from her inside-out world.
She is in the spit against the evil eye.

When I'm blue I close my eyes and see her light
coming from the Greek island in my brain
where sunflowers crook their necks, weary of time,

their wild hair burning in the sky of her wide mind.
I float naked in her color, the sea
hums in my ears, lulling me

like a baby kicking in amniotic waters.
Her throne is a transparent bowl,
a star-sapphire studded cradle of waves.

She must make love on silk sheets of air.
She must have blue skin and eyes,
her breasts amply squirting milk,

lapis lazuli looped in strands and strands
around her arms and her rounded belly.
Peaceful blue, luminous blue, keep my daughter safe.

See, she splashes her little feet in the Aegean,
reaches her hands into sky. I hug her dry
in a towel deep blue as Mary's timeless robes.

THE JUNE MY GREEK GRANDMOTHER
LAY DYING IN A QUEENS HOSPITAL

my brothers, our lovers, and I sat on the terrace on Serifos,
calling out to the owls, calling out *Who? Who? Who?*

pushing out the air and *O* of mystery from our throats,
then swallowing potent island wine, slightly sweet

and complex, while the owls called back
from their rocky home, intimate yet distant,

and taught their young to fly from cliff to cliff.
The full moon rose from the mountain's knobby knees,

rocky breasts, sleeping shoulders, and I called to the owls,
a mourning cry, a shriek or moan, a supplication

all the way to Queens—*Yiayia, live!*
though I knew *she* prayed for a quick end.

Occasionally an owl might perch on a wire above us,
keeping its body still, except the quizzical watching head.

I remember her bent head as she read or sewed,
her round owl torso, her beak of a nose,

her canny eyes, her kiss as she blessed me
with the sign of the cross and said, *my child.*

Now the moon turns our whitewashed walls to glass,
turns the night water to milk and sends its shimmer

far across the warm sea she loved to light distant islands.
When I was small I floated in her arms, hypnotized

by sun writing the dazzled alphabet on water.
Silently an owl alights on our open windowsill.

My husband takes my hand as she looks at us
and our baby sleeping between us. How large she is,

her silhouette against the moon, watching our family
steadfastly and so long I fall asleep with her still there.

She flies away unbeknown to me.
The white heat of the Greek sun wakes her gone.

MY CAREER AS A FLYER

My workshop smells of wax and ash and flesh. You can see,
      I've made my shoulderblades into feathered muscles.
Now flapping my arms, tricks shimmering on my lips like silver coins,
      angling between the shades of skyscrapers,
I'm wowed by a perfect accident: a jet flies across the full moon.
      Finding you will be like that good omen
or the dart pitched in absolute darkness, striking the bull's eye.
      Friends dance on a checkerboard floor,
and there I am, happy among the group,
      music laying firm hands on my body,
in this room yet sidling up the fire escape, taking off
      over rooftops and palms, into the panorama
of light-studded hills and freeways,
      the thousands of shadowed minds surging
white, red, white, red headlights onto and off the Bay Bridge.
      I soar into the euphoria of the wino in the Tenderloin,
who calls out, "Hey, girl! Take me home and save me!"
      If someone says, "Why don't you take a flying fuck?"
I think, Why not? Why not a flying, wet, wingéd fuck,
      our bodies iridescent among the clouds, solid life
rocking the color plane like Franz Marc's blue and red horses,
      like fleshy trees arching into each other,
dancing mud or sheets and sheets of orange silk
      flowing from the sun floating in your blue eye.
See how my body rises, the sea's pigment rising with me
      to stain my skin, and I glide blue, spiraling above
freighters and tugboats and bridges of the Bay.
      The towers wink out red warnings:
you can't help where you go, can't help flying out of yourself.
      Look up, you can see me above the city,
the wind in my mouth, the night ink on my hands.

FACE CELLS

Babies have "face cells" in their brains, whose purpose
is to recognize their mothers' facial features.

You come into the world seeing
only as far as my breast and face

for your life depends on knowing me
and there are cells in your baby brain

just for recognizing—
out of the chaos

of shadow and light—my face.
You scan me, shape me,

memorize the feathered sweep of hairline,
almond curve of eyelids,

movement of irises
looking back,

a flesh moon
rising in the room's outer space

(lips—dark, plump—
kiss, smile, coo).

You see me see you,
make me as I made you.

RAINY GHAZAL

I watch drops gather on the windowpane,
swelling up, trembling with their weight,

then shuffle off, silver elephants and snakes.
I make cities in the glass—narrow streets, a maze

of slicked stone and neon signs, a blaze
of stars radiating from water, a galaxy of rain.

Around me other girls and boys, the lesson of restraint.
Above our heads, chugging the walls, is a train,

cardboard placards of the alphabet, big *A*,
little *a*, big *B*, little *b*, each letter a face,

a character acting on the page like rain
scribbling itself on glass. Each drop has a name.

Other children tell me not to stare. Teacher explains.
They talk and language pools, pocked with rain,

and won't be a mirror. Rain, rain go away.
No, come back. I'd like to play. Fight away the shame

of being by trying to see the shape
between us, the ghost of air, the space

between the drops. What does the rain say?
Rain. Rain down rain down rain down rain down. Rain.

Your ear's on the desk, Aliki. Let your brain
rest. Let your pencil write a watery refrain.

PURPLE CROCUSES

Seduced by El Niño's eastern balm, they bloom early.
One morning they appear, sudden like shining wet paint
splashed across the newly green lawn.

They've naturalized, their opulent purples
each year more abundant with drunken bees
buzzing between six pointed petals.

Purple crocuses with shocking orange centers
were here before I stuck my shovel in this dirt,
perhaps before the old widow, Elvira Lockwood,

who dug here before me and left a wind chime
for her ghost to breathe against
while the red-throated house finches warble,

who, a neighbor woman told me, loved birds and flowers
and planted the climbing rose of pale pink and milk
that never bloomed for us until our daughter's birth.

Even as the hands touch wood, say this house is mine—
the barn, the fence, the rose trellis my love built
for the warm-petalled Joseph's coat to climb,

the dirt under my feet—these purple crocuses
spread under the fence to share themselves with neighbors,
unownable fleeting musical notes for the eye to hear.

YOU OPEN YOUR HANDS

You learned the intimate—
to recognize faces,
latch onto the breast,
cry out your pain,
smile into a smile

—and you held that knowledge close
in your strong reflexive grasp,
as if under your fingers,
those tender miniatures,
a secret lay at the center of your palm.

Now you unfist your hands
and reach into vast air,
pat flowers on the pillowcase,
fan your fingers across my breast,
find you can touch as well as be touched.

As when we two were one,
your body still nestles in mine—
(belly skin meets belly skin, eye meets eye).
Soon your fingers will pull the world
in close to taste, to see

—for you demand I turn you outward
to encounter constellations of faces,
bright slabs of window light.
Oh, small child,
all that patterns and shines mesmerizes you

and you open your hands!
I see how beautifully,
with shudders of excitement,
you enter the open cosmos—
and, in nearly invisible increments,

part from our close circle—

INEVITABLE MOVE

When I take my daughter to the Mennonite woman
who cares for her on afternoons, we pass
the old brick Groves mill, winter cornfields,

neat Pennsylvania Dutch farms, red barns
with solid stone foundations and long white louvers,
painted signs next to the mailboxes proclaiming faith:

on the way there, *Let us draw nigh unto the Lord,*
and *All things were created by God;* on the way home,
Come follow Jesus Christ and *I owe the Lord a morning song.*

The road curves like a dreamy explorer around hills,
under amicable sycamores huddled together, abreast the river,
then over it on two bridges, one steel, one stone.

In the back Zoë babbles at what she sees
through the rear windshield: treetops reach fingertips
toward the colorless sun, tin roofs glint with winter austerity.

Look, Zoë! I call, See three fat geese in the yard!
See the cows! See so many crows in the corn!
(I can't help thinking of Van Gogh's cornfield.

All this beauty will be buried soon in the dirt
of my memory, most of it for good, and Zoë will see it
not at all or in that distant home of dreaming and learning

where a door might be ajar, letting in a slit of light
but no shapes, nothing with a name.)
I wish I could stand barefoot in spring mud

and mortar stone after stone in a wall forever
and plant a Rose-of-Sharon with faith, and never leave.
If I could be like these farmers with their old brick houses,

their history and their mission, I would sing
the Lord a morning song and bless all creation
and stretch my hands toward the supernatural face.

No such luck. I kiss my baby bye bye,
be back soon. Sue holds out her hands
long-fingered and brown, smiles a lovely gap-tooth smile.

My girl flails in gentle arms and wails out her loss
as I drive away, sending up hundreds of crows,
black angels protesting over the implacable landscape.

MONTHS IN THE FROZEN WORLD

for Gerald Stern

In gorgeous, inhospitable snow, crows flap over destitute yards,
their calls tricking back the song the house made when I climbed
upstairs, as if their wings climbed the sky, as if they'd wakened
shades in that underworld, that frozen air. House music.
I'm afraid I'll say it, house music, and break the ice
when I open my savings account. I'm afraid I'll sing
to the nice teller patiently explaining how it works.
I might tell her I feel flush or ambivalent outside the public library

where ghostly books fall down the return tunnel, down there
where I stand in kitchen memory, stirring soup in a big black pot.
I might tell her my blank recollection without regret, a different house.
Grief seizes inside me. I have no choice and look out.
Do I look at the landscape and see myself? I see sun
is snow and fire on the walnut tree whose massive arms form
a comfortless circle where—shouldering air, muscular, comic, hungry—
circumspect crows span their zone with gazes and caws.

The crows. The snow. The lost house. The dream of fire.
I might tell her these months in the frozen world I dream
of fire burning all the money in the bank, lush green-blue flames.
And the bank burns, too, the house, the town, the world,
the newspapers and TVs that tell the tale of charred bills
orbiting like a billion crows over the cinders and the dead.
I might tell her of my slow free-fall toward distant ground,
that the sky blooms with twelve full moons bright

as desert sand. Blue before dawn, blue at twilight,
mournful blue, moonfull sky, the spectacle, time passing.
These are months in the frozen world.
These are things winging into nothing. See how I spiral down
leisurely like a leaf, a feather, like ashes, ashes,
like a crow laughing, you can't die if you invent your death.
I'm so happy as I plunge, telling my joke to the air—
I could spill it all to the woman asking me to sign here.

EUPHORIA AT ZERO

Euphoria is a cobalt winter sky that stings you.
A pink Cadillac fishtails 360 degrees—
then drives on. No accident.
The air deafens your skin, loud with zero and wind.
Cold is a lemon on your tongue. Bittersweet hunger.
You walk over your weaknesses
as if they were a sheet of ice,
knowing their dangers, not minding much,
confident in your big black boots.

WAVELENGTH REVELATION

I'm rowing in my small boat on electronic seas,

rowing, rowing in my glass bottomed boat.
The fish swim among holograms of celebrities
and I plunge in to join them in the ocean of news

and oldies, classical, top ten, talk and static,
drowning in radio waves.

The enormous head of consciousness looms like Buddha

over mountains of landfill rising from the shore,
microchips, television litter, radio glitter—

and the beach is tiny glass balls,
bottles, screens, test tubes shattered and worn by the sea.

Sea gulls squawk and dive in sync
with the whirling resistors sensing heat and sound.

My boat bobs in phosphorescence

and I reach for a Milky Way of flashing lights,
the control panel of the universe.

I'm rowing in my small boat on plumbless, hissing seas—

Oh, the electric weave of light, the floating seductive helixes,
the symphony of beeps and squeals, whizzes, buzzing and chirps.

Ah, the winging and winging on synthetic wind.

I'm rowing, rowing toward every horizon,
toward the edges of the screen—

Where are the palm trees? Where the dolphins?
There in that filmy glow out of which everything grows.

WITH WALT WHITMAN ON THE STATEN ISLAND FERRY

I sat at ease with Walt on the ferry,
and let my knee lean against his thigh.

An expert in corn flakes, he slipped his hand between wax paper leaves,
infused the cock on the box with iridescence,

found a true word for every crunch,
and blew the words in kisses onto the lips of the crowd.

I guided his hand under my skirt
which was scripted with the looping calligraphy of the city.

He kindly fingered my crack with one hand,
unbuttoned the brown wool of his trousers with the other.

And as I arched to meet him,
he hooked his head on my shoulder, breathing in my ear,

"Jesus Kennedy—Jack Christ—
your social memory began in 1963,

with equal parts dread and ecstasy,"
and I saw my boot on the sidewalk, the bright hopscotch chalk,

the November leaves blown against the fence,
heard the kids calling out, "The President's dead!"

Walt and I knelt on a bed of newspapers,
moaning the holy names, shuddering with the ferry engine,

as the statue of liberty, Ellis Island, and the Jersey skyline
floated by with mercury-lighted clouds.

And when it was over, he eyed the grapefruit mounds
of young men's asses, hoisted his bag of books,

and melded into the crowd, into Manhattan.
I followed, staring hard into the place

where Walt Whitman had been,
where yellow flashes of taxis curved by Battery Park

and the lighted windows of skyscrapers stretched
disembodied into the heavenless night.

BATHING JESUS

If he were a word made flesh I would want to wake him from his godliness
and wash his godliness from him as I bathe his feet in my laughing tears
and dry them with my heat and hair and anoint the topography of his head
      with euphoric oil
and comb his beard with electric fingers and pull his face close to mine
to see the multitudes in the pores in his skin, God's intricate human
      handiwork in his cheek.
Jesus would see the flame in my eye burning in time's skull, deep as the first
      breath that lighted the Milky Way.
I would pull the shirt from his shoulders and the shirt from mine
until our garments lay on the floor, cloth lungs pulsing
      with the curtain's white muslin and the little breezes
      coming in the window, everything alive,
even the wood floor under our feet warm with the oak's broad and
      branching spirit.
And I would pour warm water on his back and thighs and wake the man in him,
wake his hand reaching for my flushed and water-slicked arm, his palm
      singeing the place below my collarbone,
make him taste each word on my tongue, each complex mix of sweet
      and bitter and sour and salt
and make him sing out from his body, *the lips, the tongue, the throat,*
      the heart, the blood, all the traveling heats of flesh. Praise them.

THE TRAIN TO THE MILLENNIUM

I got an uptown train to the end of the twentieth century.
All my lovers were there, grim as hell, hair spiked with fire,

sexier than sex. I wanted to feel their life-blood strain forward
in the palm of my hand, dig shiny black high-heels into their asses

and make them scream. All my friends were laughing,
our reflections floating in the windows—over brick tenements,

warehouses, garbage, sad smashed cars in junkyards, slag-heaps,
the mowed lawns and token trees of tract homes.

I wanted to love them with my tongue as I never had before.
All the children I never had, all their friends, all my friends' children

ran down the aisles and climbed over the seats, calling out new words,
sweet and cool as apple juice slipping down my throat.

All my family, all my teachers rode with me to the end of the line,
to the enormous station where the tracks stopped,

where windows rose five stories and opened
to a field uninterrupted by the human, to the big peachy afternoon sun,

the new moon above like an ironic smile.
All our dogs were there among the cone flowers and cosmos,

retrieving calendars and dropping them at our feet.
All my students were stoned, milling about, taking in the fractured

station window light, not demonstrating, looking just like those who did.
All the TVs were stacked against a wall, turned on and tuned in

to different channels, entrancing our retinas with the past:
"Beavis and Butthead," "Bewitched," warclips, a boot to a head.

All the typewriters and computers, the obsolete and state of the art,
hung out against the opposite wall, ready to light up, bring on

the next sentence. "Fuck the world!" I called out,
like the crazies on the street below my apartment in San Francisco,

"It's over! The end!" Then I thought, it's the middle not the end,
just another day, and all my friends became strangers carrying briefcases,

women in long coats and white tennis shoes,
kids feeling their bodies under black leather.

"Goodbye," I said to no one. "Goodbye," I said
to the trains moving away on infinite tracks,

heavy with their own weight of steel, their load of people,
newspapers, umbrellas, sandwiches, memory.

STAGE

The sign says STAGE as if to name the summer street
on which Saturday night revelers trip out of bars,
call out, bump against each other, and laugh too loud
as they step over white line markers
into newly washed and gassed-up trucks.

Stage as if to frame this pain that will fade
into the ink of memory's script
like these lightly dressed people who make appearances
then disappear into the wings like the drunk's tires
screeching above the stereo bass and raging muffler,

then leave the night quiet encompassing

the closed department store called STAGE
and the mind divided, sorting its hidden merchandise
into compartments—passion in a flame dress,
caress of silk falling away, sweaty shirt, sad socks,
shoes of betrayal, a cruel wide belt,
perfumes called hope, devotion, obsession, and misery.

YOU WILL

You will be jealous and hear nothing but jealous, jealous.
You will throw yourself at your lover's feet and beg.
You will pray to Jesus though you don't believe he's God's son.
You will neither eat nor sleep. Your teeth will chatter
and you will rub together chilled hands in ninety degree heat.
You will have the runs as your body tries to shit out the toxin of betrayal.
You will flee home, feeling you have none.
Pain will blind you and you will crash your car.
You will get back on the road and a car will pass you
with vanity plates reading HURT 1.
You will will your will and it will help briefly and briefly again.
You will spin the wheel of karma and count your burdens.
You will hold your baby and weep and bless life.
You will curse the flat landscape, the walls of August corn,
praise the hills climbing from the Mississippi.
You will become small. You will become large.
You will be afraid to speak but rage will speak you.
You will disappear. You will will yourself become will-less.
Your love will speak you. You will speak you.
You will open your mouth and grow many arms and legs.
You will make love, come, call out, cry, each spiraling inside each,
a tango of hair and limbs and rage and tenderness.
You will hear all your lover's music, the high chimes of the soul,
the rhyme of the low animal moan.

WILD WITH IT

I am your underground river, flowing in the dark
beneath the earth's skin, and I am your blood.

I am the Mississippi, lighted and calm,
and the grassy hills clambering from its waters,

and I am your Mississippi flooding its banks, a volcano
flaming the sky to ash, a tidal wave. Because of you,

I am a Greek island redolent with oregano and thyme,
dry salt air. I am the sea voluptuous against your naked thighs,

the sunlight drying the blond hairs on your legs and arms.
I am your sun burning away all sight except its own light,

a sun throbbing, giving the land color and shape,
the little whitewashed house, the bed below the window full

of mountains breathing deep into the earth, bones of knees,
elbows, flesh of breasts and cocks, cunts and shoulders,

broad chest where the heart beats and makes the capers
and daisies tremble, all the nerves, thistles and sticks,

electric and telephone wires buzzing on your flesh.
I am the moonlight showing you how the sea's body stretches

all the way to New York, to streets whitened by oil and rain,
to shoes scuffing the sidewalks, and windows bright

with pots and pans dangling from the ceiling,
lovers and families, bathrooms—a guy's bent head

as he fills the bowl—I am pens, notebooks, computer screens,
I am your world wide web, I am your easy chair—

you hold a book on your knee—mine is the bare belly
appearing before the shade goes down and mine is

the kiss deepening to a bite on your neck.
I am your witch poking pins into a voodoo doll.

She who comes between us I will burn, bury, break,
shoot off in a rocket to the nothing of space.

I am I am I am. And in you I am, for you erase
and make new our two conjugating shapes.

MY GHOST LOOKS FOR YOU

My ghost hangs out on the sidewalk in Wilmington
where the boulevard leads from the highway to your old neighborhood.
She's shuffling past the station where we gassed up our cars
to see each other.
Her shirt is inside out and her socks don't match.
She's smeared a paste of kisses and come and tears
on her face and hair.
She's painted her lips and lined her eyes with the ink of your pen.
My black bra crowns her head.
She muddies her shoes on the banks of the Brandywine river,
feeds Canada geese the bread of her body,
drunk on the wine of your love.
The autumn sky is a blue bowl cracked with thin clouds.
She lies on the ground and waits
for winter, for the full moon
to frost streets and signs and houses with its sexual light.
There below the broad-trunked oak we made love in glassy air,
your leather jacket creaking a little,
your tender hand beneath my neck,
roots digging their thumbs into my back,
mist of our breathing glowing under a moon-slicked
mandala of branches, shiver of limbs, map of intimate nerves.
She stands outside the building where once you lived,
cocks her head to read the titles of your books,
lies on the bed where you tied me with the gold cord of trust
as raindrops slapped fallen leaves.
She sails out across the window of rain,
its wind-spackled sea, shimmies
up a telephone pole, tightropes across its wires,
and surveys the highways we traveled to leave all this
and find ourselves here,
within driving distance from the end of the earth.

DIGRESSIONS

When I walk into this Minnesota truckstop,
and he slides his sweet ass across red vinyl
to sit beside me, I contemplate
how I might use him to settle the score
with you. Our baby busily rubs sugar
against the table's swirled Formica surface
and pulls open packages of grape jelly
and paints her face purple, as he tells me
I intrigue him. How about I fuck this trucker,
our daughter sleeping in the cab's front seat,
us moaning on the little bed in back.
Or maybe I'd say drive just drive and I'd
suck him and he would twist his wrist to rub
my clit and the semi's magic fingers
would vibrate us to rapture. Now he lets
me know he's got me pegged, some kind of artist,
some grown-up hippie-chick, who's got the done-
drugs glow. I guess the ghosts of Blake and Ginsberg
are peeking out my ears. I guess my past
bounds out to thwart my plain Midwest disguise.
He cannot know back then I tried to be
a man, to prove I could outdrink, outdose
myself with LSD, outfuck them all.
I made my anthem "Love the one you're with,"
all that optimistic victorious
reveling in the now, so I could make
my travel plans, so I could always be
two places at once. Listen, what if I
let my leg lean against his? What if I
let my finger outline his rose tattoo?
What if I wake up his forearm's skin?
I can see you fall into the abyss—
I kiss oblivion. Bye-bye, bye-bye.
Our girl's arranged florets of scrambled egg
and toast around the floor beneath her chair,
and I collect our things, tip big, and leave,
my headlights aiming downhill, down the dark

interstate—interstate—good word to name
digression—down the banks to black waters,
the Mississippi—I'm driving this road,
a common road my design was to avoid.
I hold you in me wherever I go,
and I, not you, am keeper of the faith.

HER FACE

I see her face in my mind's eye though I've never seen her face.
I hear her voice speaking to you of her home, the testimonials
of her life, the lives that went before, of her love for you
before she knew you. She knows your history, the small town
in Pennsylvania, the father who left, the mother who lay still
in sorrow, who kissed you between the eyes and opened
the eye inside, the blind grandfather who took you inside his mind
so you heard how to make light rainbow through the blinds,
how to make the smooth curve of the chair's arm gleam cherry,
how to make your words become clay, then to breathe movement
into your array of figurines. I see her face as surely as your story—
before you knew me, you woke to see your estranged lover making love
with another in the globe of your night mind. She called you forth
with the other inside her. I see her face for I have lain in bed
when we were apart and have spiraled out of my body to find you,
to touch the moon's face with my face, feel his cool cheek
shining light into your eyes. I have watched your closed eyes,
the quick little dance of the lids as you dream. I see her face
the way I used to see my own in you, my face in you called forth.

MY SWEET NOTHINGS

Do you taste me
        on his lips? Smell me
                on his skin? How good
I am when you kiss him
        and disclose our secrets.
              You feel the art
of my experienced hand, don't you?
        When your palm slides down his chest
              you learn the way to follow
the same slippery path
        he traces on my body, my length
              of thigh, curve of neck.
And do you lift my hairs from his sweater,
        to coil around your finger
             and slide up your sleeve?
Any part of me is a prized memento,
        for I am all over him, my musk
             in each of his pores, scent of our years.
Do you savor my voice
        in the quiet sighs between
             his words? How delicious I sound,
my cells caught between your teeth,
        my spice thrilling your taste buds.
            You've known me through him,
so tell me, my lover's lover—
        even now as this tart ink
            stains your tongue—
how much you like to take me in your mouth.

WILD WIND

I listen to the wind lecture across the northern plains
but it's not content. It rubs its shoulders
against the house—I guess it wants
to be understood, wants to slink
across the sky with lightning, that glamour queen,
wants to be one with it all, the sexy one, the warbler.
So it belts out a vibrato, then hardens itself,
yowling through storm windows, making the walls
of the house and the bed where I lie tremble.
And now it sobs. Why won't it stop
bellowing frustration? Calm down. Grow warm.
Settle into a murmur like our voices talking in the night,
though all the while, beyond will, I am wild for you.

SURGERY

The sunset surgeon makes a dire incision
        into the chest of the sky, reveals organs
                pulsing in the cavity of the self.
Soon night will come carrying an armful of stars,
        that wide bandage, the Milky Way.
                Where will I be in the darkness? Will I see
my soul's shape as I lie blinking
        at shadowy bedroom blinds?
                Will I scrutinize my anatomy?
An organ for each emotion? Will I hold
        a healing balm in my hand or find the nurse
                who will take my pulse, blood pressure,
temperature, inject me with the correct drugs—
        just enough poison to kill my disease
                yet let the body fight back,
just enough pain killer to numb me
        yet let me keep my eyes open
                and find a will.
Kiss my arms, these empty arms, my belly
        hollowed out by woe. The skin of my thighs
                misses yours. Kiss my head, my face,
this wanting place and each of my eyes
        staring West at the stark hilless landscape.
                Kiss my scars, the gash where I love you.
Kiss me wherever you can,
        wherever my soul might be.
                Kiss me here, where it hurts.

LOVE ASLEEP

Tonight when you hold me in your sleep,
                I know you love me again.

Did you ever stop or did I stop
                knowing or was your love asleep, asleep

as the body in pain, though morphine numbed,
                rages against the brain's involuntary messages,

as the mind rages against the body for hurting,
                against the union indivisible, the union

cracked? Was your love asleep?
                Did your love become the restless dreamer

who encounters our emotions risen,
                incarnate, carousing the city with painted faces

and their sequined boas glistening?
                Did you see them beat their enormous purple wings

and flash their private parts
                from trench coats made of ink? Perhaps you left

for some inhospitable place and I tried to follow.
                The dark soothed my eyes yet I strained

to see through the obscure blue, to see through
                the bright slash where you strode away

and streetlights cracked the night,
                glass shards splintering out in circles.

If I reached you, you shook off my hand or
                turned your back or held my gaze

too briefly before you disappeared,
                leaving me while your body stayed, terribly familiar.

I lay down, sliced down the center, and babbled knowing
                    I babbled, making word sounds that were

not words, raving from half the split, the mouth
                    loosing syllables that craved meaning.

Tonight you hold me
                    in your sleep, yes, and I dare not

move for fear of waking you.
                    Yes, you hold me in your sleep,

your warm palm on my forehead.
                    Our heated bodies spiral around each other in sleep—

healing sleep, reviving sleep, delicious sleep, sleep that cannot lie—

ICON

You lay our daughter on the carpet
and tickle her and I laugh
for joy, for her joy and yours,

for a pure moment not suppressed by my sadness
as before when you threw her in the air,
and she looked at me to share her child glee

and I remembered to smile
and why I had to remember to smile,
to chant a nursery rhyme or play.

You and I and our child laugh together
and my thoughts are not
betrayals of the moment, are not

mirrors of your love withdrawn,
a face to face infinite regression
of reflections that even now are gone.

I TAKE THE STATEN ISLAND FERRY TO MEET YOU IN THE CITY

"Come here," she says in Texas drawl. "Come see."
Tourists lean against the rail of the Staten Island Ferry,
pull up their hoods against even the balmy November air,
    dance a cold dance on the deck.

She points quarter-activated binoculars at the Lady's torch and crown,
at the lights of Manhattan, skyscrapers rising from a core of night,
a diamond silently shooting stars and rainbows onto a shadowed wall.
    "Ya gotta see this."

"You assume and assume wrong," says man to boyfriend.
"Heard wrong. I didn't say that."
    I guess the water's hissing now.

I guess the water's lapping it up with its cat's tongue.
"Hurry up," says Texas. "I got a quarter for ya. Look! Focus."
    He complies, passionless, won't make her happy,

won't see the city in her eyes, won't feel her turned on
by the wind's rough skin on her face or the surge in her limbs

as she scales blazing towers. "Listen! This is not a postcard.
Not a photograph. You'll never see it like this."
    She spins toward him, then away,
    her red coat a cape that would tempt a bull

if there were one, if he weren't a roly-poly guy in a silly hunter's hat,
shuffling a little. "Okay," says boyfriend, "Okay."

And the two men look out toward Manhattan, forearms on the rail,
hands in prayer, muscular asses identically cocked.

The quarter moon glows between the Statue of Liberty
and the mirror-moon shaped arc of the Bayonne Bridge's blue lights.

Last time I saw you you said you were glad I came. Last time
you said I looked gorgeous in my coat. Midnight blue.
    I look good in night colors, I guess,

with taxis speeding down Houston and lit-up signs telling the truth,
how to be beautiful, be up-to-the minute stylish, stay healthy,
buy jewels as talismans for eternal love or dial 1-800-DIVORCE.
      Yeah, they make you want

to climb up to those slicked blow-job lips and straddle them
and fuck them until perfection and fucking be them.
      How will it be now, my love? After the crowds

rub against my midnight coat, after the city air blends in my blush
so you can't tell my healthy cheeks are make-believe.
      When you pull me to you on the street

where people and cars pass by fast, solid then ghost,
and when you kiss me as you have so many times in our marriage,
what will you see? Will you see diamonds everywhere?
      Streetlights, lighted windows, headlights,
      our eyes returning the light?

LOOKING BACK WITH THE ANGELS

Night comes early for the solstice is nearly here.
The sun hooks its orange chin on the shoulders of Nebraska,
then slips below the world and leaves embers and coals.

A squirrel—they're all fat now—runs high in the branches
of the elms and oaks and chestnuts that mesh over
the red sky. Our Christmas tree lights blink hypnotically

around the Indonesian angel, candy canes, wooden trains,
and polished papier-mâché apples. *All is calm, all is bright,*
I chant to myself as if the carols were piped in

from elsewhere, as if my inner space were an airport
or a department store. *Yeah, right,* I come back remembering
our fights and the woman whom you once called a blessing.

In the dopey choir of my mind a hundred radio angels
lament cheating hearts. And there are angels everywhere,
in all the colored lights ringing trees and fences and houses,

in the nativity scenes, one whose wings span the tips
of the new moon and one looking over my shoulder,
whispering by turns good words, wishes of peace,

and curses, curses. *All is never-ending,* she says,
Words, acts can never be taken back. And she casts me
into the hell where the people's heads twist cruelly backward,

and they stride backward because deprived of forward vision,
where her face is your obsession—you hate me
and I hate my face in the mirror obscured by her blond light.

Now you say love me. You're upstairs bathing our daughter.
Yet I'm stuck in a painful torque, looking back. Be an angel,
untwist me and face me forward toward you. Guide me out.

WALKING AROUND SANTA CRUZ

—Did I tell you I lived a while on Seabright Avenue?
And all night listened to the sea lions
making the dark go purple with their moans.
I was alone, nothing was familiar, no one was.
At daybreak I walked to the beach, carrying my shoes
in one hand, feeling the sidewalk bite the soles of my feet.
Sometimes the sky was blue, precise, almost shrill,
demanding I look at all the details: eaves of houses,
window moldings, texture of stucco, the succulents
whose names I didn't know blooming in the beds,
the pampas grass's haughty plumes.
The ocean was macho, rough, waves reached
muscular fists high before breaking with a clap.

Santa Cruz was so beautiful I was bitter
about the beach parties and dance clubs and bars
and wondering whom I wanted, if I were wanted.
I was tired of men talking to me about astrology
or spirulina or James Joyce or Pablo Neruda,
then not delivering the goods. I was tired
of the tease—Stevie Wonder's Inner Visions
coiling heat around dancers swaying in sand,
all of us high on expertly bred sinsemilla,
and the music spiraling in the smoke of a bonfire
made from redwood that drifted down
the San Lorenzo River in winter storms.

A man taught me the names of the pepper tree
and cormorant and the lapis flowering bush,
ceanothus. See and know this
was my mnemonic. He said, "I love you."
Four days later he was gone.
He said, "I'm a seller of dreams."
Seems I spent hours a day wandering around,
conjuring up a friend I'd run into before it happened
just to test the squeaking doorhinges of clairvoyance.
—Could I enter there? Could I dream you into being?

A woman in orange told me of the New Age,
each tooth in her smile shining forth,
as if her face were a neon sign advertising promise.
I climbed the stairs of the St. George Hotel,
held the rail painted black, counted
my sandpaper steps against the wood as air rose,
a hard globe in my throat, the invisible world
of despair swelling. I made her
my hope. Her room stank of smoke.
She lay on a ratty futon. —Why are you here?
I looked at the books stacked against the walls,
at the walls a grimy color I couldn't name.

Outside I walked in the rain, past the bookstore,
the coffee roasting company, the Catalyst—the club
nicknamed the Cattle Lust where I met
a man and a woman who took me home
and tried to take me to bed. I was tired
of being a woman, of the venomous environment,
of umbrellas, of worrying—Is my bellybutton sexy?

The storms washed away West Cliff Drive,
washed away the restaurants and stores
on Capitola Beach, and I kept walking around
day and night, past the Coconut Grove Motel,
the surfers and tourists, down to the boardwalk
to listen to the roller coaster's clattering slats,
the screams I could hear from far away,
the moans of the sea lions I heard in my room
on Seabright Avenue—now that I've found you
and lost you and found you again, did I tell you?

Do you remember the early days, lying in bed,
telling each other postcards of our biographies?
I can see lights of the roller coaster
chasing each other in helixes, the ocean beyond,
pelicans swooping up supper from the waves,
the homeless under the bridges, stroking dogs.
I can see myself in yoga class hanging from rope

upside down. Maybe the blood in my head
would turn my third eye into matter,
so I could see the future and know to hang on
until you saw me and knew me.

My neighbor believed she could read the signs
in the woods, could watch the animals
and predict the date of the Big One, the quake
that would crack the holy cross into smithereens—
Mother Earth having multiple orgasms, she said.
When she was wrong, she lit some candles
in the corners of her house, burned some sage,
closed her eyes and fists, opened them
and found new numbers inscribed in her palm.
I closed my eyes and found nothing in my hands,
only my yearning, only my long lifeline.

FROM BLUE EARTH (2004)

SKY BURIAL

Snowlands Hotel. Before dawn in one of the dormitories
David Zung is up first, moving from bed to bed waking us gently.
We mount our clanky Flying Pigeon bikes and ride out of town

on the dusty road, telling each other our dreams.
Travelers' word is if a fire's burning there will be a burial.
The fire burns. We park our bicycles by a shallow river

and roll up our pants. Water so icy that I bend over
on the opposite shore, breathing slowly, coaxing my feet
from their pain. Already the silhouette of vultures

gathering on the mountain above us. A monk in yellow robes
bright in the half-light chants, hits a tambourine and cymbal.
A young woman in an animal-skin coat nurses a child,

the boy and girl beside her talk and laugh like spectators
at a Chinese soccer game. An older man spins something
like a large, long, extravagantly decorated hat atop a broomstick,

colored rings and ribbons rising up, chiming, and relaxing
with each turn. Now some men stamp out the fire and cross
to a large boulder where they undo two squarish bundles.

Two corpses roll out in fetal position, naked,
their gender and age unintelligible. Laying them out
on their bellies, the six men start their work. Sun

begins to show us color on the ridges of the mountains,
spreading, illuminating this rocky valley
where starting at the necks the corpses are skinned,

the sheets of skin tossed to the men behind,
who cut them into small squares;
the muscles are pulled from bone, limbs disjointed from body,

bones crushed in a white powder with a rock.
It is like a butcher shop. Pounding, hacking, slapping.
Hundreds of vultures wait on the rocks or circle

or—swooping down to the boulder too early—are shooed away
by the corpse-cutters. I cringe when they get to the feet,
and keep looking back to my bicycle, which is delicate,

dark, pretty by the whitened river. By now sky is light;
the city is awake: trucks and tractors rumble,
loudspeakers have resumed broadcasting political homilies.

I pass my waterbottle to friends. Some of us sit alone and stare.
Some of us hold each other. A few look through binoculars.
Everything is clicking, rhythmic:

chanting, the voices directing from the central government,
chopping, the river hissing, vultures gliding or preening,
small, reverent, nervous, or revolted gestures of tourists.

Supports and resistances move. At least for now and perhaps
for a while afterward I can discard my fears
or walk around them, like furniture.

I will be dismembered, insensible, incomprehensible—
but, lucky accident, my flesh aches and lusts.
At last the corpse-cutter wraps the head in a cloth,

holds it up to the sky, prays, places it in a hollow,
and smashes it with a rock.
Two others cross to the flat where we stand

and drive us back a few steps. Bloody hands and bloody knives.
One of them taps me with his blade.
I check my sleeve for a stain, but I'm clean.

I've read the ground here, frozen most of the year,
is no good for burial. There's too little timber for cremation.
The body means nothing when the soul is gone.

Sometimes the Tibetans leave their dead
in a river to be eaten by fish.
We say dust to dust. This is flesh to flesh.

Vultures, symbols of peace,
the carnivore self that does not kill,
circle huge, horrible, beautiful, black-white in the blue,

the white Vs of their bodies and their wingtips' feathers
spread my fingers against a sky
the turquoise that Tibetans wear. The vultures eat.

I must get my visa at the Nepalese consulate.
As we ride back together Anna says, "I felt we were no better
than the vultures." "Really?" I say. I'm enjoying

the view of the Potala, people selling their wares,
my legs peddling, the clanking bike, the sun on my face.
I search for some guilt, but find nothing—

only this happiness, wind, elation, breath, circling.

Lhasa, Tibet

SEEN FROM MY WINDOW IN SAN FRANCISCO

Morning fog flattens the city.
    Alexander pesters two women,
        particularly the fatter one in a red sweater
who leans into the street
    to see if the bus is coming yet.
        Alexander jabs his index finger into air,
as if he were jabbing the flesh
    in her unbecoming sweater.
        He's probably saying, "Goddamn cocksucker!"
the way he always does, in rhythm,
    hard consonants too hard, 's' spit out
        so you can't forget the meaning.
Leaning into the street again,
    commiserating with her friend,
        she tries to ignore him.
But now she's lost her temper.
    She must be saying, "Leave us alone!"
        or "Go to Hell!"
and she shakes
    her plastic shopping bag for emphasis.
        She's spoken Alexander's language.
He stalks off toward Faye's Cleaners
    and comes back fresh with new material.
        Can't she tell he's crazy?
Of course, I don't like to talk to him either,
    though he's not all bile.
        One day in the laundromat he brought Nancy
(the one who yells, "Fuck the world!"
  at five in the morning)
    some cheese and crackers, because,
he said, "I'm your friend."
  And now she's sitting in a doorway
    watching him.

At last the bus arrives. The sun comes out,
    is new paint on the Victorians,
        restores them with shadow and volume.

Alexander watches the bus climb Eighteenth
    and mimes the driver steering,
        swaggering like Charlie Chaplin,
calling out to delivery trucks,
    buses, cars.
        He speaks gently to forlorn Nancy
while she finishes her coffee,
    gathers her wraps,
        walks away, saying nothing.
He stoops in the doorway and collects her garbage,
    crosses after her a few paces behind,
his unshaven face contracting,
    the pointed nose reaching almost to his underbite,
        the jaw working out words
 as silently the streetlight flashes from WAIT to WALK.

SPIRALS

When I was a child I dreamt my mother died.
Afterward I couldn't watch television.
To sit in front of that wooden box

where anything could happen brought back the dream.
The Twilight Zone was especially awful,
the way a child could run away fast down

a dark street and still fall into another world.
Sometimes I amused myself with my mother's stockings,
a fur coat and handkerchiefs that were my grandmother's,

old cloisonné compacts and lipsticks, all family
treasures I'd found before, like the books I read
again and again, familiar yet surprising plots.

But always I forgot where not to look and found
the earrings lying in the pink plush of her jewelry box,
two black onyx tear drops surrounded by silver spirals

that made me sick to my stomach, like spinning around
too long looking at the sky, then falling down
with my gut spiraling into my eyes. It was *Vertigo,*

Jimmy Stewart at San Juan Bautista looking down
the tower stairwell that rushed toward him and away,
the curl spiraling at the back of Kim Novak's head

as she looked at the painting of the curl spiraling
at the back of a dead woman's head.
So in my dark closet and wrapped in blankets I sat

with my head against my knees thinking the universe
had to end, but beyond any ending I could imagine
was more space, another universe. I couldn't stop

thinking about the universe which was so large
it blacked out the world. Here is my model
for everything I don't understand, for insomnia,

for my grandfather folding his coat, taking off his hat,
sailing from a rooftop to the asphalt of Colorado Springs,
for my uncle taking pills, having lunch with his daughter,

then lying down to die. Here are the far away lovers.
All of them. Here are two black tears surrounded
by silver spirals which I took from my mother's box

without asking—I knew she wouldn't mind. I would say
they bring me close to her. They don't. They are tokens—
beautiful and well-made—of my fear. They could be

stupid postcards that say, "Wish you were here,"
and the earrings swing from my ears almost painfully,
heavy silver and stone.

STREET NAMES

I read all the street names as we drove to visit him, wondering
who named them, remembering older neighborhoods in Bloomington,

where quiet maples arch over brick streets.

I listed them—Atwater, Woodlawn, Hunter, Hawthorne, Park—
on my way home from school. And around every corner

of thought, the night we took Bill to the hospital.

The attendant brought the wheelchair, asked, *Where is the sick man?*
Bill said, *I'm not him,* as we attempted to ease him in.

There's no ease in the changed eyes of a man with cancer in his brain.

She said his thoughts went one-two-one. No three.
The mind was compressed, helplessly enfolding malignant darkness.

He explained the picture wheel. Wheel is my word.

He drew the wheel in hospital air.
When the pictures went bad he used to know to wait

and make them good again. Now he couldn't. He began to cry.

Daily he greeted my mother in a coat and tie: *It's time to go home.*
He'd walk her to the hospital parking lot and invite her to sneak away.

They were inevitably subject to betrayal.

Before we knew, we spent an afternoon on a friend's houseboat.
Bill watched Mom and me swim from boat to boat.

He made sexy jokes and giggled, comfortable in his chair.

It was late May. I took some photographs. Houseboat, houseboat.
The deck off the cabin was like a little porch. In Indiana in late May

we have crickets and a galaxy of fireflies in the fields.

We ate chicken, drank no wine, and watched the sun set over the lake.
I hung my head out the car window to feel the evening breeze.

I read all the names of the familiar streets, just as today I list them—
—Atwater, Woodlawn, Hunter, Hawthorne, Park—a prayer against
seeing them populated with no one I now love or recalling my dream

that the day we were told comes again. Tired of crying,

she takes a shower. I watch her undress. She is over sixty
and has a beautiful body, my mother's body.

She says, *You and I belong to different worlds. In my world people die.*

It's only a dream, but it's a cruel thing for a mother to do.
It's true. I can't cross over to where she is.

I am her child and as her daughter I am to be her child. One-two-one.

THE BLACK ROOM

Then the night was black black.
When I was in that room, I was in deep.
I could pass for eighteen in the bars
when I wore the right clothes.

A boy and I took sleeping bags to a field.
Red clay stuck in the grooves of our shoes.
It was wet around us and we each
put a hand in the other's jeans.

I wondered how to breathe,
and hung on to the edge.
Afterwards alone I pushed
right over it thinking about all the circles

our bodies made in the muddy field.
All this time I was thinking how
to live my life, how I would not
be like my parents, how I would.

With no one but a boy I knew
even then didn't matter much and no experience
of my own, I was trying to decide
how to make it happy.

Sometimes I couldn't stay in that room
though I'd painted it all black
with a few stars and moons. I liked it.
The summer leafy and light at the windows

and the walls' darkness wrinkled by that light.
I took my dog deep in the woods
or lay face down in the grass smelling
all the summers of my childhood in it,

making a jungle of the blades.
Or walked around town barefoot with nothing
but a dime for a phone call
in the change pocket of my jeans,

even if it were the middle of the night
and everything asleep but the crickets.
The drunks had shouted their last shouts,
leaving the bar. Whoever was going to make it

in a car had, and was looking out the window.
The moon and Venus chased each other
across the mountain ridges, danced a moment
with their reflections,

and the lake's chest breathed slowly.
Then the car's headlights
pushed uphill into the pine grove
and disappeared.

Whatever it was that forced me out I called
despair. I looked at my dirty bare feet
on the pavement and thought, I'm just going
from one black room inside to another outside.

I tried to picture whom to risk my dime on
to reach, relishing the desire—
as now I imagine why I wanted
to walk it off, wanted to walk away.

A DECLINING NEIGHBORHOOD

If you pay attention to all the random events
in the news, if you imagine a map of the city,
plotting where everyone in an alley

with a knife is, and if you place yourself
in your small rooms, the front and back stairways
are prospects of violation and escape.

Everyone in a window is looking out and in,
not looking out for you,
only looking.

You pray you hide your thoughts
well enough to be legal and send your manuscripts
to several friends for safe keeping,

hoping they are friends still.
You blamed it on the goatee, sign of bad intent,
that he briefly wore—yet you can't forget

his eye burning orange despite tender gestures.
You closed your eyes to close out his, feeling guilty
for the betrayal, for making him a mere sensation.

You can't put together
why the surfaces are good and white
while cockroaches breed behind the walls,

why you are sorry he makes you miserable,
sorrier he makes you happy. You are sorry for him.
You watch him from the window as he goes to work.

A Doberman barks at him through his chainlink fence.
All day long the crackling as kids set off fireworks
and they set garbage on fire to make fire-engines scream.

That crazy guy next door clanging and clanging
before his garage full of junk is straightening out nails,
for Christ's sake. You sit inside listening to each one,

identifying your neighbors' thumpings on the stairs,
waiting for his steps, then the welcome snap of the deadbolt.
You can't wait for him to make you safe again.

THE IRISES OF THE MIDWEST

In winter, sun is a crab burning
through black tree lace as the strict god
of country churches breathes in a headful
of ice. Snowy restraint. Yet spring's
a stain of iris beds that can't
be washed from the linens. Then sky
shrinks into a malevolent
blue eye while sinful petals bloom.

ON THE HOTTEST SAN FRANCISCO DAY IN RECORDED HISTORY, HE PLAYS PIANO AND SHE LISTENS

She recognizes the music her grandmother used to play.
Once, when the girl took lessons,
her grandmother played a piece by Mozart
that the child had stumbled through
not understanding its potential.

The grandmother played so beautifully
the girl leaned her head against the piano
and sobbed as if for inevitable disappointment.

It is quiet and hot all around the music.

How light-headed she feels—dry heat pushing her
into some clear, unexpected blue place
where newspapers identify currents of the soul:

record heats that will be superseded by new ones,
surprise aftershocks of the quake that was not the big one.

She can hear her grandmother saying,
"One thing in my life I'm happy about—
I fell in love only once."

Though as a child she learned to doubt her grandmother
who told fictions, sometimes to awe her
and sometimes to frighten her into good behavior,

the woman believes her, that she fell in love only once,
that when the handsome captain
first came to her family's home in Constantinople,

her grandmother arrived finally and fully in her heart.
Though he has been dead longer than they were married,
she still calls out, "Vassili!" in her sleep. The woman listening

remembers a dream—in the transport of lovemaking
she asked, "Why can't it be like this forever?"
and her lover replied, "If it were forever, it wouldn't be this."
She knows she is all the characters in her dream.

She can't find a place for her heart to stay;
she can't find a place in her heart to stay.

She watches the man's back as he plays.
All the child's pain seems written on his back, all
the movements of his fingers are notes on his back

and his arms are like wings, she thinks.
She cannot think what the music is like,
only that, light in the heat, happy and sad,
it rests nowhere as if it could be like this forever.

A NIGHT IN ROME

It was a day of brides.
This morning in the hilltop town of Orvieto
was a wedding we didn't see—just rice

on cobblestones and people lingering—
and one we did see in the grand cathedral
with its black and white marble stripes,

gold inlay and godly heights, the story
of Christ and his angels flying in frescoes
about her and the groom (whose too long trousers

pooled at his ankles). "Look, oh, look!"
we called out on the night bus to the city.
There was the Colosseum lit up and a grassy hill

where hand-in-hand running, climbing,
shimmering in the headlights,
were the bride, lifting her skirts, and the groom.

Our hotel is near the train station
in the old red light district of Rome.
Five flights up with suitcases.

We've eaten prosciutto, asiago, and walnut bread.
Hot green olives washed down with Chianti
from a six hundred year old cellar in Tuscany.

Everything good to eat and good to say.
You lie on the bed; I stand
at the window and report:

a woman's taking off her clothes;
with her back to me she smiles
at her reflection.

No, it's a man, not a mirror,
and he's smiling at her.
Now you stand by me and spy.

Now we lie down and darken the room.
All the various warmths of making love,
(everything kisses).

Coming and crying,
as if it were new. *As if it were new,*
we think, and not now

and we were not returning to a place we know.
In the dark I listen to strange music.
The percussion of your heartbeat

and your breath, the little gusts on my forehead,
someone in the hall rattles a key, a drama on TV,
traffic, the two-pitched emergency sirens,

something I can't identify echoing in the airshaft.
Not a wind or a voice.
Not the lover's words sighing,

Angel and *Darling.* Not me
praying for your safety and perpetual return.
Under my ear, your chest rises and sinks and rises.

How fragile! I think, not believing it.
Everything passing like the repetition of
I love you. "Strange sounds," you say,

just as I thought you'd dozed off.
In a room that's contained many passions,
we marry again.

And we're talking, showering, dressing,
locking the room, passing
the Colosseum, walking for hours in Rome.

BLUE EARTH

The moving van slowed uphill under my possessions:
jewels, lifework, junkboxes.
The turtle with the world on its back.

Mile markers rushed by.
The truck crossed the Missouri River into the Midwest,
and I left California's promise.

Just when I thought, "There will be no more,"
I saw a sign, BLUE EARTH. A town perhaps
named over a century ago

by someone who could see the earth from space,
a Winnebago holy man who prophesied
the moonshot photograph.

Then I guess the land was stolen by settlers
who counted blessings in corn flourishing lush
blue in the haze and summer storms.

Affliction was the twister that ripped away a wall
but left the Afghan hanging on the rocker-back,
every dish in the hutch intact.

And then snow came,
the sky cleared,
and the fields turned blue again.

I imagine the faithful filing into church
to kneel and clasp their hands in the awkward pews,
then to bear witness to the commonplace in the graveyard.

I don't know how they broke the frozen earth for the dead.
Now I see my old life everywhere it isn't. Here
the lakes tell me brightly how the light looks:

now in all the *ohs* the sun reflects on water—
then my awe becomes a history,
open-ended as loss, and I need

to make it like something I see:
white barnsides in the morning
next to rectangular black fields just like billboards

advertising WHITE and BLACK
or the real billboard exhorting, PRAY! IT WORKS!
as I drive to work.

My soul under winter, my sad sleep
are like black dirt
and corn stubble,

or the white farmhouse and the white barn
lit up unlikely, like *hope* or *home,*
the white house and the white barn followed

by another house and barn that almost seem to yearn.
Just when I thought "There will be no more," I saw
Blue Earth. Hope, harvest, stubble, title of my days.

WINTER AND WAR ON LAKE MONONA

I call my dear friend Edwin Honig
because winter is a burden to me.
It is like an ice block on each shoulder,
all the muscles tightening around my heart.

He says his college days in Madison
almost took his manhood. We laugh.
And he advises I buy a few pink
light bulbs to shed warm light around me

and start a story about our phone call
in which the student who read a newspaper
in my class is the same one I discover
fishing in an icc hut on Lake Monona.

Then I will have started a splendid event.
Indeed, who is this boy-man
who follows world affairs in spite of me
and my books? He sits alone

on the ice with a bottle of vodka
and he reads that yesterday the Iraqis
bombed Tel Aviv, the coalition forces
destroyed a hydro-electric plant

and a factory that, depending on who's
reporting, manufactures baby formula
or biological weapons. It is so cold
that we look at each other with tears

in our eyes. I think how tough he is,
patiently drinking as he guards the hole
in the ice, as his father and uncles did.
Every few minutes we hear warnings

on the weather channel: prolonged exposure
to cold can lead to irrational thinking
and death. Yet here he does for sport
what before was done for survival,

as if one could be impervious to the elements.
"Good boy, good boy, good boy,"
my student says as he bends to pet my dog.
What will *this* man do? He shows me pictures

of tortured POWs. I show him the box
of pink light bulbs I've bought.
Then we stand together a little embarrassed,
the tears freezing on our cheeks.

I carry home my fragile load,
and when I turn on the lights
—oh, splendid event!—
the white walls are warm like flesh.

MORE THAN A MONTH OF GRAY WINTER IN MADISON

No one says, "What a beautiful day!
The sky is so gray!"
So why should I feel bad for feeling bad
when the whole city is pale

as if God had stretched out a cold wet rag,
then clamped it down with his enormous thumb.
And would it be easier if I had faith in God,
as the early settlers did? They understood

gratitude. The soil here is good, supremely good.
He ordered the seasons: the black earth rests
in winter, delivers its reward in summer.
And it is good to separate good from evil,

the now from the future, to know the virtue
of suffering without despair—
though newspaper articles and the stiff photographs
from the 1890s depict madness and suicide:

children lying before the family hearth, side by side
in caskets; the woman in the swamp,
grinning wide, her arms arched above her head,
snakes tight in her grasp.

She held their vileness high for the lens to record.
Today the local comic-strips joke
about our collective north winter blues.
Windows iced-over and dim

make sense of the saying, darkness closes in.
The sun sinks at four and we're Mad City,
not the Madison named for the luminary democrat.
Atop the capitol the gold goddess of progress

almost gleams already frozen in the gray sky
while below her a roller-blader glides
beside the not-yet-frozen lake.
He moves fast but his lunges are slow,

graceful, easy, propelled by powerful muscles
and something in his dogged, forward posture.
From the sidewalk I'll soar into spring,
I guess, on still icy silver wings.

SADNESS

Rilke says sadness is the moment the future enters us
by surprise and pushes us into the unknown.
The handsome bartender says, "Your drinks are on me"
—and leans across the counter— "What'll it be?"

Alcohol is heat in my ears as I catch my reflection
in the mirror, happy flirting without forethought.
But days later alone the question comes back:
What *will* it be?

and I remember moments with you
when time raced quickly around us like a romping young dog
and we were amused. Today time reminds me of the hound
knowingly guarding the underworld. Sadness slips in—

doesn't it?—even in the gentle pleasures of the body
which pass too and remind us of loss.
Rilke says be attentive and patient with sadness
because it is our way of learning through solitude.

In your eyes I see your solitude watching mine.
I note the line in your cheek when you smile.
Our sad fate enters me—when we are sad together
or sad apart, how attentive and patient will we be?

BLUE ROOM, BLUE HORSE

The doctors don't know why it hurts, so I ride
    it out, as ordered, take pills for help, and ride
a galloping blue horse around the world's circumference,
    through the starving hands in Somalia patiently
holding out their bowls. My head-weight clangs
    against my collarbone and voices say it's hell
as the blue hooves clamor down broken halls
    of Bosnian nursing homes while the dogs of the underworld
howl with the sirens howling their intent to help.

The flickering light hurts my eyes and the horse won't stop.
    I can't listen to the authorities debate solutions.
It's mid-August, warm, still.
    Blue curtains filter twilight onto white walls, blue.
Outside, trees are blue bouquets lined up on the horizon.
    When everything shadows blue, what *was*
is not, is a haze over fear yet is clear,
    a blue, glazed bowl inside a blue bowl circling
inside my aching head. What is it?

Are physical ailments an echo of emotions
    and a headache the price of doubt or fear
or suffering with those suffering on TV?
    Or is it that blow to my head, months ago,
when I was hit, my packages lifted slowly by nothing
    out of my arms, then the crack of my head on pavement,
and the membrane around my brain weakened
    permanently, as they explain in science magazines,
which I can't read right now while the room is turning blue.

It is a sign from the body: the impatient, hungry,
    blue horse galloping pain into my head,
turning the room bluer. The names
    of the sky and the sea seem also to be
the beginning of darkness or the color of veins.
    Prussian, ultramarine, cerulean, cobalt, cornflower,
and indigo unreadably shift on my hands as I write—

through the clattering bowls comes the wild, blue horse!

DREAM WITH BILLIE HOLIDAY

In dreams East is West.
                              I squat beside a tide pool,
feeling the anemone close around my finger. Cliff-spray flies
with the gulls and I'm with a lover I haven't seen
in decades. That first night,

                                             hearing her
voice
in the dark room as if hands stroked my whole body
and the dark were night waves,
I was quiet but overcome by something like what holds
waves up a moment
so high before the boom and sibilance.
"Who's this?" I asked. "Billie Holiday," he said.

Now it's much the same;
his body still wiry, his hair still black,
he bends bare-chested over his guitar.
                                        I only see
the years intervene in the expression on his face.
At last I say, "We weren't so nice to each other."
"I've heard that complaint before," he answers, a bit resigned.
"I meant me," I say, "I wasn't so nice."
                                   Then to punctuate
the half-lie I press my palms into the small of his back.
And I hear waves breaking in my hair, in the pillow,

and in our illicit kiss.
Back then we kissed and told,
                                  so all our kisses were new.
When he slept with a dental hygienist who slept with the
dentist, he smiled ironically, playing his thin fingers
across my hip as if it were his guitar.
                                   I saw a swan
floating in each of his teeth and wondered
                                             why the god
transformed himself into a gaudy, stupid bird,
                                        why his eyes

were green as the new leaves outside the window.
Even as I wanted him all the more,
the swan enraged a memory
of his learned bragging—

                          he read only the old poets

and thought all the new bad. So

                         I was bad. One morning I

came to him. I kissed his neck

                            and he kissed mine and

found an illegible haiku there. "Tell," he said.
"No." "Tell," he pleaded. "No," I laughed.

Decades later in a place we never were,
we are as wild as we were that morning. I hear
sea lions moan from the boulders and piers

                            and the room is loud

with ocean and the moon-face
fills the window with an open-mouthed sigh.

Then I see Billie Holiday standing in the door,
mock-shocked, laughing behind her hand, singing,
    I've been seen with someone new,
    But does that mean I'm untrue?

                                Then I'm back.
It is the January thaw in Wisconsin. The sunlight tricked me.
I stood beneath sunny but frozen buds and remembered
something. I stopped myself where this dream began.

GREEK EASTER

All the Greeks in Bloomington come here,
to Peter Costas's for Easter. Whole garbage cans
of roasted lamb
beside long tables of food, and ingredients—feta, filo,
olives—ordered from faraway Chicago.

We say, *"Kalo Pascha."*

Vassili pinches both my cheeks and says, *"Koritsáki mou."*
We click our eggs together
and the holder of the unbroken egg gets luck.
I ask my mother, "Why are all the eggs for Greek Easter red?"
"The red is the red of Christ's blood
and of the lamb's blood." "That's sad."
"Yes," she answers "but the eggs are for new life."

She doesn't say Christ died for our sins, she never will,
though the neighborhood kids say my whole family
will go to hell for not going to church on Sundays.

To me, equal to Christ's story is the story of "that Helen,"
who was beautiful
and ran away to Troy in spite of marriage and kin.
The sorrows, the strategies, the triumphs of the gods—
each is a red egg
piled high in a bowl.

I walk under the grape arbor, which is still in winter.
At dusk dancing begins.
My father leaps and turns in the air, arms spread
like island windmill sails. Then he holds the handkerchief
for my mother to lead, quick-footed and laughing.

My parents are beautiful. I wonder if they love each other,
though I'm sure they do, I'm not sure I believe what I see—

I go inside and sit with Doctor Frank.
His voice is calming, deep and slow.
Then I go outside and see
smoke and a small fire backlighting the corner of the yard
where my brothers and some other boys
compete to pee the highest, broadest arc.

I look at my white shoes. I can smell the delicious lamb.

BROTHERS

One brother sleep-walked in the garden,
looking for father. The other dreamed the dragon
fire-red with seven horns and ten heads.

But now my parents were together again
and we five traveled from the Greek mainland
to island and island, temple and church.

Many people on Patmos were cross-eyed
as if their vision were cursed by revelation.
A woman showed us the Cave of the Apocalypse,

the two hollows in the stone wall, silver-haloed,
where John laid his head and his hand, dreamed
shared suffering and kingdom and endurance.

She owned the only restaurant open
that time of year, took a liking to me, fed me
a delicious breakfast before we left,

then sat across the table talking as I ate.
I was neither child nor adolescent.
She saw the child in a way that comforted me

and made me sad to say goodbye.
Winter and stormy—we left on a fishing boat,
the horizon lost to waves. Again and again,

the bucket with a line tied to its handle
was tossed puke-filled into the sea,
then retrieved scoured by turbulence.

When I retell the story to my brothers,
I say I left the cabin's smelly misery
and lay in the life-raft, cool air an elixir,

my stomach pleasantly full. I was the only one
not sick and for the first time saw dolphins
rise up like waves out of the waves.

Funny how both my brothers also remember
the life-raft, dolphins, and being the only one not sick,
as if one could not suffer the others' suffering.

THE FERRY TO SERIFOS

The horizon slides up and down as the ship rocks
on mild summer waters. Slightly sickening.
Relentless memory and worry. As if there were a crack
in my brain like this wake churning white
in the sea's restful darkness. I doze and wake,
doze and wake. Can't tell whether it's dark
or light that agitates me. Gulls follow.
Above, luminous edges of pumping wings.
Below, they glide along the water's surface,
mimicking the dark fluttering in small waves,
swooping across the horizon like a song,
like a sustained voice, rising, falling.

At last I see Serifos, lovely beyond memory.
Ancient terraces, relics of cultivation,
meticulously lace the hillsides and hold narrow fields
of light. Rust of iron ore, gray-green rocks,
purple blooming herbs, olive and ochre grasses:
all complex but modest colors of the land
responding to the sea's vivacious blue.
The village is a white crown.
My house is up there, in need of a whitewash, no doubt.
Blue windows and blue door. Cool tile floor.
I'll climb the village stairs and swim in the sea.
Health. Clarity. Hope. Everything like the blue light
of sea and sky augmenting each other,
the somber rocks and ebullient daisies
and red poppies. A warmth calms my temples
as I lean on the rail, looking. Then shouts
of sailors handling line, anchors and chains clanking.
I gather my bags, stand with the others, and wait to land.

COUNTING TIME ON KÍMOLOS

Two months ago his brother wrote
  "I want the simplest of funerals"
    and swallowed a bottle of pills.
Now my father and I arrive at the decaying port
   where the small ship and the cement slab dock
     dominate a cafe,
a few flaking whitewashed houses,
  and a rocky quarter-moon beach.
    Eight tourists on the whole island.
Old women drive donkeys overwhelmed by wheat.
  An ancient urn still balances on a solitary pillar.
    The slats of shutters hang unpainted and askew.

This is not a happy island like Sifnos
  known for its excellent cuisine,
    its garbanzo bean soup
and a salad
  of fresh white *mizithra*
    sprinkled on a rose of tomatoes.
There the port is lighted
  with strings of bare bulbs
    and the waiters bring carafes of local wine
to full seaside tables.
  Here it's forty-five minutes wait
    for an unsavory *souvlaki.*

But we are told, Go to the *paniyiri.*
  In celebration of school's end
    teenagers do local and ancient dances
led by their elegant teacher,
  and his precise
    and passionate feet.
Relatives eat at windy tables.
  Children run in and out of the winding maze
    or climb on stage and repeatedly jump off,
untiring and unscolded.
  Watchers join in the dance,
    motivated by no apparent cue.

My father jokes that he too is part-Greek:
    "I'm related to Greeks by blood,
        after all, my children are Greeks."
Forty years ago against the wishes of families,
    my parents married and lived on the islands.
      My father learned the captain's dance,
to spin as he leapt high slapping his feet,
    then nearly falling,
        to recover
at the crucial second
    Opa! people cried,
      and threw plates to the floor.

Manos Hadzidakis, he remembers, told him
    Western music comes to a climax and ends,
      while Eastern music goes on,
sustained passion...some people get up to dance,
    others sit down, and the dance continues
      as my father takes my arm. We walk back
to the hotel in dim light. Ghosts of whitewash
    float up from darkened houses
      and white calla lilies float
above the simple pine box.
    Behind us is a celebration, music sustained,
      and dance—*Opa!*—whose end we will not see.

PLEASURE ATTAINED MORBIDLY, HARMFULLY

In Greek "kamaki" means harpoon. It also refers
to the young men who sit down with women in cafes
and press them with invitations
or sigh, "Sssss," or "Mounaki mou," my little cunt.
Yiannis, a notorious kamaki, a real fisherman,
takes women out in his boat, watches as they swim.
Later, at his sister's restaurant, he keeps
their wine glasses never empty and never full,
feeds them morsels from his catch. Today he sits with me,
"You're a woman who likes to be alone.
You go to the beach alone, you listen to your music alone,
and now you're going to your house to be alone.
Why don't you stay here?" He wants me to stay in the port,
where the discos and bars are,
but wherever we are, he says, there is a party.
The bus comes. "You're a strange woman," he says.
I ride up the mountain thinking I am strange.
I ask the priest sitting in the square how he is.
"Old and sick, my child." And he blesses me,
"*Doxa to Theo.*" And asks after my grandmother and mother,
my father and brothers; he sends them greetings
and blesses them and blesses me again.
He doesn't know what I will do after I shut the door.

As my bathwater boils I read Cavafy.
He records that Imenos admonishes us "to love even more
pleasure attained morbidly, harmfully;
the body rarely feels what pleasure wants."

I pour hot water on myself, freeing my skin
from the salty tightness of the sea—
but the sun still burns in me,
soft and clean, alert with longing.
A stranger can kiss your neck and make you all cunt,
but that's not what sensual pleasure requires,
it's not attained morbidly, harmfully enough.
That stupid man, with his table full of laughing

and flushed women, telling me who I am
as if his words could keep me speared and writhing.
He has an instinct for mere violation.
I could spit with scorn, like the priest's mad daughter.
But what is it? Is it Cavafy's despair?
"He's lost him completely. And now he tries to find
his lips in the lips of each new lover."
Is it going back and back to some imagined first place?
there where talking, gentle and gentled,
the body understood that *ekstasis*
is a being put out of its place.

GO TO THE GOOD AND RETURN WITH THE GOOD

When I left Serifos an hour ago,
    Kiría Mariniá stood in Halídas's store,
her jaw shaking, and said slowly,
    Go to the good and return with the good.
On the islands, more than in Athens and other cities,
    people keep their greetings and farewells:
blessings and good wishes for every time of day
    and year, for health, a trip, appetite,
a swim, and the long life of children.
    Go to the bakery or across the ocean,
and they say, *Sto kaló.* To the good.

It's good to remember that those who say
    the islands are isolated are mistaken.
Islands aren't self-sufficient and never were.
    The old men sit all afternoon in the *kafenéion*
playing gin rummy and backgammon,
    smoking, drinking Greek coffee or ouzo,
and eating *mezedes*—small plates of cucumber,
    olives, feta, and cubes of bread
topped with sardines, all stuck with toothpicks.
    Everything savored slowly, slowly.
Sigá, Sigá. They can always tell you
    when the boats come and from where.

At each docking a crowd gathers to see
    who's returned, with whom, and how many tourists.
In the ancient commerce between the islands
    friends and family depart and arrive,
to go to Athens or to fish. Lovers separate
    and in the journey there might be another.
There's always the possibility of return.

At the ferry's stern I watch goodbye a long time.
    Look back, look back to the night village—
window lights gathered at the mountain summit
    and the lighthouse rhythmically

rolling its Cyclops eye, recalling that on Serifos
    Odysseus blinded the one-eyed monster,
whose dark head might float below
    the agitated wake. On my tongue is
tangy sea air—*wanderlust, luxury, tender, commerce.*
    Will the words ferry me to the other side?
Go to the good and return with the good?
    Lights of other shores, other
ships rise from the horizon, and I sail on,
    look back until the island—
then the lighthouse—disappear, loved.

New Poems (2004–2008)

Pique

A Verse Drama

PRELUDE

ON THE ROCKS

I'm floating in sea exactly the same temperature
as the flesh of the man between my thighs,
as the breasts of the woman whose length slides

upon mine, our limbs undulating with the seaweed below.
I'm lucky Pierre and nothing matters here,

except that our pretty *ménage a trois* balances

three glasses of scotch on the rocks on our chests,
like sea otters with oysters and clams. Languid,
we keep one hand free

to raise our drinks to our lips,
pass an ice cube from tongue to tongue,
and mix salt water with spit and alcohol,

I grin and pronounce what a sweet word kinky is.

Ah, the night sea—how good it is to be
horny and drunk. Nothing matters now

that I've ruined so much on the faraway shore.

What were those brilliantly mean words I said?
Seems the same smoky taste smoldered on my tongue

when my anger came,
and now the same
heat presses pelvis against pelvis.

And how did I forget the secret I forgot
was secret? I guess I betrayed a friend

who's not my friend now.

I can hardly recall a hurt look or my love's face
who caught me with the wrong love—poor wronged love—
because the artful moonlight glosses my skin,

friendly strangers keep me safe from my memories,

and at the moment I'm toweling myself dry,
wrapping myself in a silk sarong.

We're so pretty,
we'll be fucking again at dawn.

Mmm, mmm, mmm...
magic alcohol—ruin the past and give me now,
and do it now, give me

whatever I want, whatever I want, whatever I want.

THE HEADACHE

The past three days a headache has laid me
        on my back to dream beyond metaphor
                what better to do in my position.
In apartment buildings all around, dogs on balconies
        practice a chorus of longing, mounting
                when the ambulance howls
My urgency is an emergency! Or maybe, because I'm prone
        on the bed, the siren summons
              Eros! Thanatos!

Some kid's been playing a stoned
        three-note riff on his electric guitar, a drone
                louder than the dogs. Oh, lord, his wah-wah
replicates my headache's throb. He'll need a larger
        repertoire to get laid, though he's probably built
                like Poseidon raising his trident,
a university student from Crete,
        where the men are gorgeous
              and notorious.

I'm the picnic on the beach blanket,
        a little middle-aged—but so what—
              I'm adored by the demigods
who surround me, black hair wet,
        kelp striped across their chests,
              a salty taste on their skin.
Just when I've made myself a porn star,
        the phone rings on cue
              and I see you, my blond love,
emerging from the surf,
        jealous of my frolic, ruining the scene.
              Don't you know I'm a girl and love too much?

My head aches. The boy's serenade wavers and stops.
        He's made a girl's giggle ascend
                into a shriek rousing the dogs.

If only I could hang up,
        don facemask and earplugs
                and tune you out of my dreams—
if only I were a blithe boy, like you,
        unattached to the sex images
                stored on my hard-drive—
I'd prefer even the dogs yowling
        and the kid's noodling on his guitar
                to your baritone voice.

11:11

Eleven-eleven. The intimate minute.
In eleven one mirrors one. At eleven-eleven
you sigh in sleep;
I blink before dream,

and see two prime numbers face to face, indivisible:
I prime + *you* prime = entwined for all time.

Or is 11:11 like a fence between
two neighboring couples talking
back and forth, two and two,
even and divisible?

I can't help myself recounting
and recounting again: you looked across
our hours and minutes and saw in a flash

a common denominator between you and her.
I know, who doesn't shift one's gaze
a minute or more to some other,
fantasize spending a lovely eleventh hour?

Now alone in my head, I count the odd and even wee hours past twelve.

Though I'm odd, too old to squeal *wee wee wee* all the way home,

I'm even enough to grasp that my *I* stays beside your *I*
while who knows the hot numbers you dream of?

And do you worry too? In a minute you could be the one
alone, finding me, whom you thought was the one, two-timing.

Or when the clock blinked midnight,

did you see how 1
stands lonely when 2
glows on, and the sum is 3
on one side of the equation,

and on the other: zero-zero.

Once we were in eleven-heaven,
eleven-eleven abed.

We were all
the ones and onces

I can't help enumerating.

Remember eleven-eleven comes again.
It's almost a threat.

Pique

LISTEN TO THAT CRAZY GHOST

Listen to that crazy ghost—   she'd drive even a saint
like you to drink,   the way she lurks
around the kitchen,   follows you to your desk.

A cricket no one   else can hear
nestles between her   brain and skull:

You want quiet to contemplate   some larger pain,
but she taunts you,   *Hey, angel, you're no angel!*
And you're not donning robes!   You're a slug
wearing a smelly flannel bathrobe   all the live-long day.

Could be the synapses   have gone loopy
because her meds ran out,   because a cricket croons
you-hoo drink-ink   too-whoo much-much.

In the past she heard   crickets outside
the glass. Now she wonders,   were they
outside or were they hidden   in the nerves?

Well, *you-hoo, hello-oh,*   it's all your fault—all *you*
if the glasses in the cupboard   are magic,
for they reappear   taller after they break.
One drink a broken day   is bigger each day and the next.

Listen, you tell her again,   there's no damned cricket.
It's the clock hiccupping   from one second to the next.
It's the Little Owl, *Athene Noctua,*   whose hoot carries
a message from the goddess   in a code you can't crack.

(Sometimes you forget   all the promises you made.
You don't believe the story   she tells you about you.)

You're long-suffering.   Anyone will testify
who made you   wrap three pints in off-season clothes,
made you hide them way back   in the coat closet.
Why an ugly lamp fell from the top shelf,   bruised your head.

Who stays up too late, rattles   office supplies on your desk,
who counts up the bottles in the trash,   who dumps

half-melted ice cubes and   watered-down scotch
down down   the drain with an angry clink
that almost smashes   your treasured tumbler.

It's the ghost who drives you crazy   (oh, faultless you).
Tell the bitch *shut up.*   Have another drink.

THE CRAZY GHOST FEELS BETRAYED

The crazy ghost feels betrayed, cannot sleep,
    takes a pill, drinks a bottle of wine,
        although she's a lightweight.

She leaves home, buys cigarettes,
    although she does not smoke. She lights up
        to better suffer her baroque marriage.

The crazy ghost wanders the late night city,
    mindless, in danger, to find the graveyard
        where she belongs, an unheard joke.

Under coppery street lamps men gossip
    beside their delivery trucks in the cemetery parking lot
        bordered by florists who cater to mourners.

She bravely makes out ghosts of trucks, men
    with two heads or three, with multiple arms,
        each man like a tree. She's seeing double-triple, that's all.

She ponders the one who's blonder, why
    her husband squanders his love, responds to her.
        What a quandary. What gobbledygook,

she mutters to a cat glaring from the dumpster,
    a delicate chicken bone in its jaw.
        Here city-kitty, pretty-witty—oh fuck!

have some pity on me. The crazy ghost stumbles
    by the stuccoed wall, where evergreen cypresses
        are dedicated to reminding

the living what forever might mean. The bitch
    lies down on winter ground. *Why does he want*
        to talk to her when he walks in the wind? Why not me?

Why does he think me shrill? Is it a sin I'm not
    new, a thrill? I'll lie quiet until the rhyming
        dizziness from pills and drink subsides.

No one can see a ghost. She feels the dirt
    on her cheek, curls her spine, brings knees to breasts.
        For an interval she does not care to see.

Why not pass out, pass away for an hour or so?
    Then she will have assigned some worth to herself,
        dead to him as she is, a crazy ghost

babbling outside the wall where others burn olive oil,
    candles, and incense, and place pictures and flowers
        in shrines to the memory of love on earth.

THE CRAZY GHOST WALKS DOWN SOPHOCLES STREET

The crazy ghost walks down Sophocles Street.
On an October morning, she asks is it fate or chance
all is well with the world or so it appears.
History is behind her: the marble for the Acropolis
came from quarries dappling Mount Penteli white.
History is before her: an old couple walks ahead.

All is well with these two or so it appears.
They stroll arm in arm, both in elegant brown wool,
she leaning on him, trusting, he holding strong.
The crazy ghost wants to grow old like them,
have a long history, like them, by fate or by chance.

On an October morning, she passes a little city church
that looks like a farmhouse: geranium and basil on the patio,
a grape arbor running from its eaves to a fence
painted the same golden-green as leaves.
All is well with the world, or so it appears.

The crazy ghost walks down Sophocles Street
where a patch of wild pink cyclamen flames beside garbage
dumped among olives, pines, bitter orange—rot, harvest, bloom.
She fell in love with a man who called her a wildflower,
but treated her like trash. Her fate or dumb chance?

The crazy ghost thinks the priest who sings the liturgy
in the garden church on Sophocles Street would have an answer.
Then by fate or chance, from the cross-street comes
black flapping robes, the priest in his columnar hat—
and all is well with the world or so it appears.

The crazy ghost walks down Sophocles Street and prays:
"Let my marriage not be tragedy, let all be well with us."
"I love him, I love him," she chants, then makes a wish
(instantly disowned) that he would disappear by fatal chance.
She sees a yellow kite caught on a wire, can't read her own script

written in fear, can't know her happiness may begin at the end—
the winter he leaves her—nor if she'll replay the drama.
She wants God to exist and make all well in the world, by fate not chance.
A red bus passes by and a woman inside crosses herself on cue.
The crazy ghost almost crosses herself, too.

THE CRAZY GHOST NEEDS A PLAN

The crazy ghost needs a plan.
      She walks in streets where she half-belongs,
      a foreign city in the Christmas season in a Christian country,
where a red shooting star lands on an apartment rooftop,
      its green and yellow tail dangling down,
      skimming the balconies below.
Plastic Santa Clauses are lit up in geranium pots
      and climb from terrace to terrace
      on ropes of colored light.
She is so lonely that she needs to be alone.
      She is tired of only being the loved hostess to guests,
      tired of not being the most-est to her love.
The crazy ghost needs a plan for the holidays—
      lipstick, so the teeth glow in her smile,
      blush, so her cheeks appear fresh.
She'll wear stretchy red velvet to show off her breasts,
      put the poison poinsettia up high,
      out of reach, a bit of color but safe.
She'll bake sugar cookies shaped like trees, stars, and bells,
      which she and her kid will decorate. She'll whip up
      some cream for the pies, laugh with foam on her lip.
Even if she's a wit, if she gives herself a rosy make-over—
      roses everywhere, between her teeth,
      behind her ear, petals on her eyelids—
the crazy ghost cannot be seen, not by the rare free taxi,
      its amber flag lit, ready for hailers,
      not by the jogger out for his ten p.m. run
or the business man home late, backing headlights
      into his garage—she is a ghost, after all,
      and she walks the darker sidewalks, dodging streetlamps.
Her glasses mist. Her ear revives the afternoon's thunderstorm.
      A little sweet mud sticks to the soles
      of her silly red sneakers, too young for middle-age.
She sits down on a bench. The green lumber is saturated, mossy,
      almost a living limb. She touches wood,
      not a cross, as if it were her own skin.

Yet he won't be charmed by her, his wife.

     Silent night.

     Except the nattering dogs make her want to howl, too.

The plan to be happy for her kid and to woo her man

        means banishing the crazy ghost and her pleas

        and needs. Why does she refuse to shut up and disappear?

THE CRAZY GHOST IS DOWN

The crazy ghost is
down,
down on her luck because her love got
down with *her,* that *she,* who went
down on him. The crazy ghost will face her
down somehow. She'll ram a pronoun
down her throat, won't deign to set
down her name. Their fling-thing will die
down. She'll wait it out, though she's having one melt
down after another. In her dressing gown gives him a dressing
down instead of a rub
down. He shouts her
down, tells her she's weighing him
down. They sit
down to the magnificent supper she cooked up as she broke
down, wishing she would burn
down the fucking house. He plays
down the other, hopes she'll quiet
down, not go for another show
down. The crazy ghost can't choke
down every perfect course, but swills
down the wine he chose with expertise. Maybe feeling let
down is one way to slim
down. He can still wolf
down his meat. He's closed
down to her raining
down her love during the winter
downpour. Used to be in the rainy season, they heated up, stripped
down, bedded
down. Deep
down she only wants to lie
down with him, simmer
down, live
down her knock
down, drag
down rage against his freezing her out. She showers
down—the only way to warm up. The crazy ghost creeps under the

down comforter, decked in flannel unsexy as a wedding gown. Cast
down, she drops
down, slows
down. Why is their love so up
down, up
down? She pulls herself up, bowed
down over the blank page, presses
down with her pen, and jots it
down, the bring you
down, the turn you
down, the crazy ghost writing all the damned downers
down.

THE CRAZY GHOST'S HUSBAND WANTS TO MAKE IT UP

The crazy ghost's husband wants to make it
up to his wife. She's cracked
up, and dreamed
up that he screwed
up with someone else. She scrunches
up her face, tensed
up. He's so good at covering
up with lies. You've got a knack for jazzing it
up. God! I want to throw
up. She knows he feels cooped
up with her. Why would he pass
up the chance to be with someone who perks
up with every word he speaks? Who conjures
up his youth, props
up his ego damaged by middle-age. The crazy ghost digs
up her husband's past, stinks
up his space with her mixed
up ideals. Just grow
up, face
up to me. Our love is higher
up, she proclaims, summing
up. C'mon, he murmurs, psyched
up, I don't want to break
up. Cheer
up. Shut
up and let me love you
up. He gets it
up. He always gets it
up, always keeps it
up. She's heated
up, hikes
up her skirt, climbs
up on his face, wants him to fill her
up. He rubs
up against her, revved
up. They finish
up, wash

up, and curl

up together. The crazy ghost's husband sees her close-

up, his wife waking

up, rising from the grave, rising

up to him,

up and

up and

up.

THE CRAZY GHOST LOSES THE USE OF HER RIGHT ARM

The crazy ghost loses the use of her right arm. Her shoulder is frozen. The weight pains her when she walks. She cannot lift her fork or glass, cannot write, cannot dress.

Her husband cuts her meat. He pours her wine. He does the dishes, wipes down the counter. He squeezes toothpaste on the brush, warms the water on the cloth, and washes her face and neck.

Gently, he slides her sleeves down her arms. He undoes her bra, lifts the straps. He unbuttons and unzips her jeans, takes off her panties, her socks. Then he lays her down.

Pills don't kill the pain. Even lying still, she whimpers—the weight, the unbearable weight of her arm. Her husband hugs her hip.

I'm sorry you're in so much pain, he whispers. The crazy ghost begins to hope again he cares for her, cares she aches and cannot sleep, cares she has a body.

In the morning, after she showers, he dries her body, touches her every part with the towel. He dresses her again, and smoothes her hair, helpless as she is. She wants him to stay with her, to bring her tea and stroke her cheek. He helps her to the couch, spreads a throw upon her legs, hands her a book.

And then he leaves, as is usual now. Her ghost follows his daily path, onto the train, up the steep city hill, and into another bed. Day after day, her shoulder stays frozen, knowing what it knows.

THEIR HISTORY IN PIECES

Every night the crazy ghost goes back, leaving
      the wife's sleeping body. She can't help the path
            her feet lope along, to find the town

the Susquehanna River flooded, where markers
      on the street signs tell the level of the waters:
            12 feet, June 22, 1972. The flood before their time

"was bigger than the 100 year flood, the worst
      natural disaster ever to strike Pennsylvania."
            Agnes poured 18 inches of rain on PA in two days,

forecasters unable to tell how much rain was falling,
      emergency communication frozen,
            telephone lines knocked out by the storm.

Their first home was on high ground. They stood hand-in-hand
      in the basement and noted the dark line
            on the wall, showing where the flood rose,

not harming the house, yet leaving many
      to die, ruining homes and businesses
            without warning. That was before their time.

The summer they remodeled the kitchen,
      they put the refrigerator on the back porch,
            cooked on a grill outside—salmon and summer corn

from a riverside stand, picked from the stalks that day.
      She planted roses; he built an arbor for the Joseph's coat.
            She planted tomatoes and basil; he built a fence.

After the blizzard of '96 they stood together
      in the head-high snow. Then came the thaw
            and the rains fell "in excess of three inches."

They lived on high ground; others flooded. They went down
        to the basement to find again the dark line from '72
              and dry dirt beneath their feet. That was their time—

their daughter was born when the tea roses bloomed,
        an impenetrable bramble by the side of the house.
              The baby first walked on floorboards water never reached.

That was their time, before the husband took a lover,
        before the wife became the crazy ghost,
              before their emergency communication froze,

before the crazy ghost wandered the town each night
        beneath three-globed streetlights lit in the dusk,
              crossing the bridge above the river banks,

where Jack-in-the-pulpits and forget-me-nots
        grow in mud between mossy rocks.
              Unseen, her misty dress folds

and she scoops up a kitten dotted with brown fleas.
        She wants to rescue the animal, warm and clean it,
              and, dreaming a safe place, goes home,

though nightly, the roof caves in, the rotten
        floorboards thundering down,
              window glass cracking in lightning.

And she finds herself, the crazy ghost, wandering away
        from the town the past warned would flood again,
              searching after their time, out of habit,

for another ghost—the ghost of happiness.
        She sees a man walking hand-in-hand with a child,
              and she trails behind, wanting to walk with them in time.

THE CRAZY GHOST'S HUSBAND CRIES

The morning he leaves, the crazy ghost's husband
puts his palm on his wife's forehead and wakes her.
He cries and hides his eyes, his hand like a blinder on a horse.
She thinks—what are blinders for?—

when he puts his palm on her forehead and wakes her.
He sits beside her on the bed and talks.
She thinks, what are blinders for?
Oh, yes, they put blinders on horses, she recalls—

as he sits beside her on the bed and talks—
so the outside won't distract them from their path.
Oh, yes, blinders go on horses, not on men. She recalls
it's only the third time her husband's wept before her.

She's outside him, won't distract him from his path.
He puts his hand over his eyes. Then she can better see
it's only the third time her husband's wept before her
in their twelve years, and the third time

he puts his hand over his eyes to better see
another woman. He's shut his wife out
for the third and last goddamn time.
The crazy ghost no longer wants their eyes to meet.

He's found another woman. He's shut the crazy ghost out.
She buries herself beneath the comforter,
can't bear his gaze any more than he can bear hers,
yet she promises herself she'll remember all he says.

She buries herself beneath the comforter.
He speaks to her and hides his eyes. They don't converse.
Though she promises herself she'll remember all he says,
her memory is a grave and she can't dig up his words.

He speaks to her and hides his eyes. They don't converse.
The crazy ghost lies in bed, grieving that she is dead to him
for his memory is a grave. He won't dig up her words
and blind to her love, he leaves their married life.

THE CRAZY GHOST SEES THE GODDAMN MOON

The crazy ghost sees the goddamn moon,
the goddamn moon
smiling above cypresses, apartment buildings, and gloom.

She stands still in the living room,
can't bear to go into the bedroom,
and there's the goddamn moon

reminding her of the afternoon
her bridegroom
left her to exhume

her own small bones.
Oh, that doesn't rhyme.
Stupid moon

doesn't equal the afternoon
she impugned
he left too soon

after twelve stupid years.
Oh, that doesn't rhyme.
The crazy ghost can't push a broom

across the sky and sweep away the moon,
can't even assume
he loved her or when he stopped.

Oh, that doesn't rhyme.
The crazy ghost sees the goddamn moon
and moon rhymes with swoon,

and with spoon,
for two bodies attuned
to the other, so others can write bad love poems.

Oh, that doesn't rhyme.
There's the goddamned moon,
the goddamn moon

whose rays festoon
the walls of the empty doomed
goddamn fucking bedroom,

where they aren't fucking.
Oh, that doesn't rhyme.
Something is broken.

The crazy ghost sees the goddamn moon,
her memories strewn
everywhere, too many, too small, too much—

hopeless to order.

THE CRAZY GHOST DREAMS OF HOUSES

The crazy ghost dreams of houses, the house where they began,
and she glides through rain, a blur of rain, a blur of rain,

searching and chanting, Where is he? Fuck, fuck, fuck.
He won't carry her across the threshold, across the threshold

rotten floorboards collapse beneath her weightlessness,
oh, she is weightless, chanting, Fuck, fuck, fuck.

The roof is a hole, open, open to lightning, the treetops' dark mesh,
silhouette of crossbeams, silhouette of his bootlaces and jeans.

He's hanging in air, her love. He's hanging in air, her love.
The crazy ghost dreams of houses, the house where they ended,

and she glides through desert dust, dust, dust.
She looks for her love. Let's face it, the dream's meaning is

always the same: she fears death and wants to fuck, fuck, fuck.
There in the house with a wall of windows, where windows let in joy

and blue air aching with dust made weightless by wind, weightless, weightless,
he sweeps the floor covered with dust, dust of their skin cells sloughed off by age.

The crazy ghost dreams of houses, houses sold, houses and all they buy,
the supper table, cars in the garage, film, books, music for the bed, the bed,

where she wants to lie with her love, her love lying in sheets as in a shroud,
his eyes sightless, his ears plugged, her touch, her touch weightless to him.

She looks for her love. She wants to fuck, fuck, fuck.
She's a crazy ghost, and a ghost can't matter to him, isn't matter or flesh,

no matter the house, no matter if it were her home,
she can't enter again, can't cross the threshold blocked

by another woman, the woman she used to be or never was,
the woman he left or the woman he left her for.

In her dream of houses, he wants her love, wants to fuck.
The doors are blocked, the floorboards rot. Fuck. Fuck. Fuck.

THE CRAZY GHOST HEARS THE MUSIC

The crazy ghost hears the music
    he played for her
        at the start of their love,

the music he gave her so he'd be
    with her when they were apart,
        his emotional ventriloquism,

so she'd be in his small apartment and
    lie down on his bed,
        slightly chilled, and smell

the candle on the nightstand,
    burning by her head,
        and she'd smell again the scent

that his clothing still held, dropped
    on the floor when he'd stripped,
        the life of him in all

the objects in the room,
    as gently he held
        her wrist and kissed the length of her,

the candle's dim glow burnishing their skin,
    rain dripping from the windowsills—
        echoes, heartbeats.

The crazy ghost hears the music, feels him
    stroking her again.
        Him, him, him.

She hears herself sigh his name
    over and over.
        She sips his wine and

his name comes to her yet again with an off-rhyme: Oh, self.
   Oh, selves entwined
     and then—

what's the metaphor? what is
   the vehicle for distance?
     Split, cracked, broken, ripped

apart.
   All words to wound the body.
     The crazy ghost

hears the music and wonders,
   Is sex profound or merely confounding,
     the flesh continuing

the conversation or just dumb?
   The sound makes him present.
     The music answers her,

as once he did before
   he stopped.
     He was that way.

Was.
   Was.
     Was.

Now is not.
   Voice, violin, piano, and guitar are ghosts, too,
     harmonizing with the crazy ghost,

playing her
   as once she was, was, was,
     a woman loved.

THE CRAZY GHOST DREAMS OF HER PRINCE

The crazy ghost arrives at Penn Station.
In her dreams the vehicle of change is a train.
It is winter in New York, steam rising
from the manholes and her lipsticked mouth.
Of course, she wears a fur-collared coat and forties pumps.
She's in a film of her own directing.

WHEN CRAZY GHOST CASTS HER LEADING MAN

When the crazy ghost casts her leading man,
an icon, an all-powerful verb rolls up to the curb.
Look what a magical figure he cuts, entering

the scene from his vehicle's lavish interior—
a state-of-the-art limo or Darby's carriage
or the dark prince's resplendent hearse.

He bows before her with a sweep
of his fedora or his velvet cap
adorned with an erect crimson plume,

and reveals a zipper along his hairline,
inviting her to undo him,
and stuff her dreams into his it-boy head.

He takes her in his arms as he directs
the chauffeur: Drive! Drive everywhere
the city is beautiful—let us see

parks, trees arching over us in the moonroof,
rivers shadowed by night and glittering
with skyscrapers' windows

and the dazzling spans of bridges—my love
though the beauty outside can't compare
with the inside, here with you,

he whispers, and the legend presses
himself against her brocade dress.
The crazy ghost is glad for the dark,

glad for the scenes passing by the glass,
the couples arm and arm on the sidewalks,
the extravagant displays of goods in the shops.

With all the urban verve, her luxurious clothes,
and artful makeup, perhaps her prince
will see only her loveliness, her smile

returning his. Perhaps when he unzips her
and her back touches the soft leather seat,
he'll be too enthralled to notice

the crazy ghost's memories filling the cab
with their subtle special effects
and their peculiar soundtrack.

If only the story would end here, if only
the credits would roll right now, as they kiss,
the golden couple cast in Hollywood bliss.

THE CRAZY GHOST'S ACCOLADES

Ladies and gentlemen, let's have a round of applause for the crazy ghost's
many roles in service of the wife. C'mon, baby, take a bow!

With the power vested in me by claptrap, twaddle, and mumbo-jumbo,
I bestow on you, the crazy ghost, a purple heart in the marriage wars. Brava!

This lady was some brave little soldier, willing to die for the cause, a double-
agent: sex slave for the enemy while penning leaflets for the resistance.

She played the raven, the nightingale, flapping her ragged wings,
the professional mourner, her cheeks smeared with mascara and inky tears.

She gathered nettles, poison ivy, Venus fly-trap, tobacco, bittersweet nightshade,
and drank the dark potion and writhed unrequited. Ah, such bitter poetry—

she longed for her beautiful husband, and, all the while, we saw his infidelity,
that she must relinquish the stage to another leading lady.

Ladies and gentlemen, I regret to inform you of another act:
the crazy ghost must kill the wife—or better yet teach her to kill herself.

Here are the props: the blade, the vial of pills, the rooftop, the rope.
And more props: desire, faith, feeling as one and in love, just as you were taught, girlie.

Folks, think of the amazing feats we've witnessed—and let's pray this show runs forever.
Watch—I lay a huge bouquet in her pallid arms, a red rose between her teeth—Voilà!

Does not the thorn prick her lip and does she not bleed! Let's give her a big hand
for her discipline, her devotion—she performs the same script again, despite her fate.

EIGHT WEEKS AFTER HE LEAVES, THE CRAZY GHOST OPENS THE BLINDS

Eight weeks after he leaves, the crazy ghost
opens the blinds. She puts the clothes away
that she's scattered across the floor, the chair,
her drawing table, changes the grimy sheets,
and dusts the furniture. The crazy ghost

has dark and gray roots, her cut has gone ragged,
and she's inhabited her bedroom,
her tomb, from winter into spring, her hair
a fright of middle-age, a vaporous aura
of heartbreak, emanating from her brain.

Her hair stylist, a stud, shows off his bulge
as he snips, perched on the counter, servicing
her, as his T-shirt rides up his ribcage.
At home she shaves her legs. Let them be seen
again, let me not see my legs and think

they won't be seen or touched. The crazy ghost
obliterates the darkness of the room
they shared, opens the blinds and lets the light
play on the blankness of the walls, his absence,
and absence of his images. The picture

window reveals the tyranny that rules her
because she loved him, for the window is stark
and blue, and spreads its warmth indifferently
around the room and on her naked skin.
She comes again at last, her body comes

back to her again, back again the dark
and matter and the flesh, hers again to own.

INTERLUDE

INTERLUDE

She lies in his arms on the couch. Outside
        the glass door beyond the balcony
                is the park on the side of Likavitos Hill.

A ruby hummingbird and butterflies hover
        in the purple blossoms of an Easter tree
                surrounded by pines loaded with new cones,

their needles feathered by sunlight,
        their green shadow deepened
                by blue Athenian sky.

He asks her how the divorce is coming,
        about her past, her thirty years of bitter loves.
                She talks into the afternoon,

lying in his arms, unused
        to a lover's listening, inquiries, or interest.
                He smiles and winks and asks

more questions, and gentle, avuncular,
        points out her mistakes,
                delivers his wisdom.

"Look out the window at the beautiful trees."
        He strokes her until their conversation lets go
                of words.

Then he undoes his jeans,
        hoists her onto his lap,
                and enters her.

She palms the crown of his bald head,
        strokes his fringe of white hair.
                He cups her face and

his brown eyes hold hers
      as she comes
            and as they come.

"Try not to fall in love with me. That's my advice," he says.
      "Falling in love," she replies, "falling
            in crazy fucking love is biological

and designed to drive us to make mistakes,
      have children, and stay
            miserably married too long."

But she loves being with him, loves
      their once a week interludes, and dreads
            the hour they leave his calm apartment,

though she knows the interim days she also loves walking alone
      in the suburbs, in the vineyards, among wildflowers
            and olive trees, longing for him.

Her mobile rings. She answers and arranges visitation
      with her estranged husband, her lover's semen
            sticky on her thighs.

La Vita Nuova. She stands naked before the glass,
      looking out at the gorgeous park.
            Unseen, a street musician plays the accordion below—

"Never on Sunday," of course—and a woman clip-clops by in high heels.
      She's probably dressed up, on her way to meet a man,
            and soon she'll be tottering at his side, leaning

on his bent arm, allowing him to guide her, to keep her
      from tripping on the steep stairs and streets of Likavitos
            littered with dog droppings and bitter oranges.

The rapid clicking of her heels: she's in a rush to be with him,
      though the flagstone and marble sidewalks are slick.
            Crazy, she thinks, to risk hurting yourself.

OUT OF TIME

He sleeps on his belly, his fist under his cheek, a little smile, out of time
Despite wrinkles and white hair, I think he looks like a boy, out of time.

A stuffed dog on the radiator. Press his foot to make him sing "Singin' in the Rain."
He dances in his red slicker, the umbrella tick-tocking across his torso, keeping time.

He shifts, wraps his arms around me, and breathes into the back of my body.
The mirror shows us in the posture of making love, still and beyond the reach of time.

The little dog sings a happy refrain and dead Gene Kelly dances in the rain.
The man says, "Don't imagine a future with me." We kiss out of time.

An afternoon of talk, making love, talk, sleep, talk, making love. Perfect.
Perfect except listing creates a narrative and an end when we'll be out of time.

A car alarm goes off four times in an hour. His mobile rings, rings, rings again.
The apartment building door bangs too loud, and slams me out of time.

I place his palm on my belly, my hand on his: "Synchronize our breathing."
His worrisome breath—a little catch or click between the in and out of time.

We make love again. When we don't face each other, our eyes meet in the mirror.
I speak in the present tense, though the mirror and the afternoon are old, out of time.

I love his limbs at rest, his chest against my back, his arm below my neck.
His big boned wrist and a hand lie on a pillow. One day they'll be dead, out of time.

I'm turned toward the mirror in which my face is cut off from my body.
I see my bare shoulders and breasts, my hands writing in my book, out of time.

The moment I resist coming, not wanting it to end, I let myself go, trust he'll begin again.
Desire implies a future, blank as it is, the next page out of time.

THE CRAZY GHOST TELLS HER LOVER

The crazy ghost tells her lover
        she's met someone new. She holds
                her mobile to her ear in a park below the Acropolis

and looks through a wrought-iron fence
        where statues are arrayed in the ruins.
                Behind the crazy ghost, who cannot talk

without crying, two young lovers in black
        are sprawled on marble steps
                making out and feeling each other up

unmindful of the hardness on which they lie,
        as if the steps were luxurious cushions,
                as if the park's border, a narrow bed

of pines, oleander and olives
        screened their play from the walkway
                where pedestrians approach and leave the high city.

"You follow your need," says her lover
        no longer her lover, gentle
                and sage as ever.

"No, it wasn't a need!" retorts the crazy ghost,
        not giving a damn that she's weeping
                in a public place

where travelers of the world
        seek their genesis, to see and pay homage
                to Greece's greatness, now fallen.

She recalls his quiet apartment, high on the hill, private,
        the windows facing only trees,
                as if his rooms were separate

from the body of the city.
        Only he knew where she was
                when she disappeared

and entered his domain. And he held her
        against his chest and stroked her skin,
                and she returned to her body.

"You didn't call. I'm not blaming you.
        I thought your silence
                meant you were breaking up with me."

How hard it is for the crazy ghost to speak.
        "No, I don't want to break anything.
                I wanted to create a distance.

I was a passage
        from your husband to someone else.
                I could not be more."

She listens to his incorporeal voice.
        What was
                between them had no shape

and now he's helping her say goodbye
        to the erotic
                in their friendship

just as he helped her say goodbye to the crazy ghost.
        Goodbye, again, crazy ghost.
        Goodbye, again.

Together they were
        visible
                only to themselves.

"You need a man who will stand beside you."
        "No, no, no, I don't."
        He repeats her name soothingly:

"You say things about yourself
        you wish were true but aren't.
                More ghosts."

She feels something in her throat
        that she can't swallow,
                at once sorrow and joy—

joy for the thrill when her new love
        took her to lunch at an open air restaurant,
                and held her hands on the table, for anyone to see.

Then he walked her to the metro station in Constitution Square
        and they stood together, kissing goodbye
                in that public place.

THE CRAZY GHOST AND I WALK IN MAROUSI ON MAY DAY

Because spring has come, I practice speaking in the first person.
For example: the crazy ghost and I walk on May Day,
when Persephone emerges from the underworld.
No one works. People picnic, fly kites, and make wreathes.

Perhaps the crazy ghost doesn't need to speak for me. We walk,
her pointy black boots floating above the grasses.
No one works. People picnic, fly kites, and make wreathes
of yellow daisies, poppies, clover, and mallow.

Her pointy black boots floating above the grasses,
we pass my old school on our morning route
through yellow daisies, poppies, clover, and mallow.
Closed for the holiday, the Feast of Flowers.

We pass my old school on our morning route,
French now not American. The uniforms are new.
Closed for the holiday, the Feast of Flowers.
Each day I pass, a whistle blows. Kids line up on the blacktop.

The school was American, and the uniforms new, then, too.
Mornings we practiced soccer and Greek dances.
A whistle blew. We kids stood in line on the blacktop.
The flag was raised. We recited the Lord's Prayer and Hail Mary.

Mornings the children practice soccer and Greek dances,
breathing in white flowering locust and honeysuckle.
The French and Greek flags are raised and they recite prayers.
I squeeze spongy chamomile to release its scent, recalling

breathing in white flowering locust and honeysuckle.
I grieve my marriage. The crazy ghost is with me.
I squeeze the spongy chamomile to release its scent, recalling
my shoes and socks soaked with dew, my hopeless prayer,

as I grieved my parents' marriage, chanting, "the Lord is with thee."
She lifts up the hem of her black tiered skirt and says,
"Your shoes and socks are soaked with dew. Stop hopeless prayer.
You're no longer a wife. You are an I, with your own memories."

She lifts up the hem of her black tiered skirt and says,
"No longer a wife, an I, with memories before and after him.
you're Persephone emerged from the underworld.
Give up the ghost. You can speak again in the first person."

THE MORNING AFTER HE BROKE

The morning after he broke
up with me, the crazy ghost

and I traveled
to the next island.

The wind whipped up a froth
of whitecaps and sprayed seawater across

my windshield, cars and people waiting to board,
and the priests who gathered in the port.

The crazy ghost rose
from the foam,

and joked
like Aphrodite she's invoked

by broken hearts.
But a ghost's art

is to bring
her voice to any dead thing,

to make these salty sea-drops
into tears, the wind into your sobs,

your tears into cheap crystals upon your cheeks
and rhinestones on your damp sleeves.

Look at the priests on the jetty, dressed in their black best,
their big gold crosses dangling on their chests.

The Economou papou died. It's a fact.
Yet you act

as if the fathers wait here in the wind to give last rites
to your short-lived love affair. You give in to trite

cynicism now he's cut you off, shamed
you for wanting more of him, complained

in the end
your passion overwhelmed

him. I'm half a person, said he. My better half felt
you in you, then died. What's left

of me cannot understand the word heart.
Logic is my trade, my wealth, my one art,

and I argue so deftly, I make any and all take the blame.
The horn blared. Our ferry came.

The wailing mourners disembarked,
old women in black from their shoes to their headscarves,

and following them the hearse
laden with enormous wreathes,

the priests taking their places behind, their pace a slow amble,
and then more ghosts, more ghosts flew in with the seagulls:

the biologist, the lawyer, the philosopher, the narcissists,
the musician, the sculptor, the sailor, the ones who showed their fists.

And then the crazy ghost exclaimed,
Oh, lookie yonder! The relations

sailing in—right on cue—on a luxury four-masted yacht,
the extended family players enacting the plots

of our dramas, retelling and foretelling the wreck
of our lives from the upper deck:

the drowned idiot uncle, the fat acquisitive wife,
the brother who took his own life,

the mother who left her family for love and said it was money,
the son who shot his dog in agony.

Papa wants his son to buy him houses and Mama needs jewels.
Of course, they are—no—you are—no—we are—weak and cruel.

I called out *Bravo!* to the miserable cast
as they waved, bowed, and clapped,

though I didn't invite the ghosts emerge again from the mist,
thought they had vanished

for good. To make me crazy
I guess the crazy

ghost beckoned
her friends

to end upended love, to help me find an end—
I boarded the ship for the next island.

CODA

WILL THE CRAZY GHOST EVER LEAVE ME?

Will the crazy ghost ever leave me, as if I were smoke, as he did in the end?
And is she my old childhood friend, whispering in my ear like a girl in the end?

Who spoke to me quietly in the dark?—not the cypresses scraping the sky.
Not him, though I cried from the deep, hear my voice, not him who left in the end.

The crazy ghost came to me—*Deliver my soul, O Lord, from lying lips, a deceitful tongue.*
Set me free from wanting the bliss of his lips and tongue, false in word and flesh in the end.

Shall I stop bathing, wearing make-up, shaving my legs, and wearing leather shoes?
Shall I cover the mirrors with black cloth, though she was my mirror in the end?

If the crazy ghost leaves me, I'll sit on the floor for seven days, my muscles feeling her ache.
I'll eat no meat, drink no wine—no uncut fruit will nourish me, if she leaves me in the end.

Who will clean her, wrap her in a white shroud, stay with her body 'til she is in the ground?
No flowers, no music, embalming nor viewing, says the law, yet she has no body in the end.

I'll tear the cloth above my heart, my plain black blouse, if she no longer glides by my side.
Yes, she is a crazy ghost, never at rest, and perhaps *beyond any blessing or song* in the end.

What to tell the tombstone engraver, what dates and name, a pair of hands or a basin?
We seven mourners will eat hardboiled eggs for the cycle, death being birth in the end.

I can't let go of the crazy ghost: *My soul clings to the dust: revive me according to your word.*
When he forsook me, I thought I had died, but through her, I, Aliki, lived in the end.

EVA'S VOICE

POEMS OF AN IMAGINARY POET

MARKET SONG

c'mon ladies c'mon girls
      come taste my olives my little black pearls
c'mon come buy greens from my fields
      hey my eyes hey my soul forget your grief
everything's fresh fresh fresh
      I've got arugula and spinach leaf
freesia red lettuce celery parsley basil dill
      I've got the best quality hey little girls
the best deals if you will buy from me
      wheel your cart over here my sweetheart
just picked today today today
      rosy grapes black grapes green grapes
once we Greeks were slaves
      now we've escaped all that
hey lovely girls look all's so good
      once our lives in Greece were poor
look here fresh fruit right off the tree
      smell my oranges my sweet pears
three kinds of apples
      and sticky black figs
c'mon ladies c'mon good wives
      come to my stall look at all I have
sharpest knives mops and brooms
      coffee pots and socks
dustbins dish towels and tablecloths
      underwear t-shirts blouses beautiful scarves
hey ladies hey girls once all of us starved
      and what did you eat today and what will you cook
come look I have flowers flowers flowers
      c'mon my golden one my soul my eyes
see these pinks in pots for your garden
      they attract butterflies
come take my flowers for your table
      I picked them today today today
no more slaves no more lies
      c'mon darling c'mon my soul
eat my souvlaki hot from the coals

listen my sweethearts my golden ones
long ago soldiers showed you their guns
        and took your jewels in the busiest city square
hey ladies hey little girls
        today all's for sale in the open air

THE BLUE HOUSE

I can see a long way up here
where the blue house is balanced
on a bluff yellow with late summer
fields that extend to the city.

You can see me, for the door
and the windows are open to air.

I sit in a chair and hold a cup
of tea. Or is that you I see inside
and is that me, running downhill,
away from the house, on the path

lined with hip-high wheat.
Looming larger above me

the closer I come is the jumble
of buildings, a white cross atop
each sky-blue dome, the church
enclosed by Byzantine battlements.

Is that figure below the cathedral,
almost too small to see,

raising an arm toward the city
in joy? Or turning back
to wave goodbye to the house?
Why does the modest cottage

seem so isolated from town?
Why is it painted such a radiant blue?

The wood looks like the glass
of the evil eye, and the planes
aren't square, but ramshackle.
The foundation is shored up

against the hill, on the brink—
I can see the danger now.

And yet the blue house
invites us to look in, enter,
have a seat and drink
a cup of tea that tastes

too beautiful on the tongue
when you exclaim, "Ah, the view!"

The house was not blue.
My memory painted it
the color of the morning sea.
Look, out there, far from shore,

the fisherman is
disappearing in his orange boat

that floats along a gray smear
of light, marring the sapphire depths.
In the impossible pigment
is the day we have to leave

for good, to find other refuge.
No, the blue house was not

a hue in nature, sea or sky
or a precious stone.
It was a color made
by human hands, like a home.

THE DESTRUCTION OF THE JEWISH GRAVEYARD, THESSALONIKI, 1942

In the churches with our tombstones mortared in the walls,
let the priests speak in tongues and let them sing

the psalms in Hebrew, not Greek. When they kiss the icons,
let their lips touch the lips of great-grandmother Miriam,

while, haloed in gold-leaf and hammered silver, Uncle Isaac
smiles his gentle half-smile. Let the painted wood, the polished

and sweet flesh of baby Jesus be the image of cousin Jak at eleven months,
son of Anna and David, born and died in 1912.

Let Herr Dr. Merten float on his back in his swimming pool, so he won't see
the inscriptions rippling on the walls, only the sky above him

cloudless and windless and utterly peaceful, the pool compact and still.
From the corner of his eye, he'll see the maid holding a tray

arrayed with steins of amber beer. Her starched apron is so bright,
a sun shines on her belly. Yet let him have no calm. Let him feel

incessantly the waters of the Danube pull him down
with the 5,000 who drowned on their way to Treblinka.

Let those who cross a threshold carved with letters of the dead
enter their homes and let the smells of cooking enter them:

oregano and dill, lemon and thyme, lentils and tomato, chicken
and chick pea, olive oil, capers, and parsley, sesame seed and honey.

Then they will remember we Greeks starved together.
And beneath the opulent scents of our shared cuisine,

let them smell a little gas leaking from the stove, just a little
poison gas, not enough to harm them in any way.

Then in the distance, maybe they'll hear a train heading north.
Then again in the distance, they'll hear another train heading north.

Let the professors and students in the university hear their footsteps
echoing in the marble halls above the bones of half a million of our souls.

Let them hear our music and dance in their shoes scuffing the floor.
Let the rhythm haunt them with a dream of our history

that does not appear in their books. And let them hear our names,
Zacho, Beni, Janna, ring out beneath their heels, *Rebecca, Allegra, Vital.*

Let them hear the families, *Kohen, Perera, Molho,*
once carved in stone, *Russo, Torres, Ben-Ruby.*

Let them read our names, *Abraham, Bella, Bienvenida*, between the words
giving them the knowledge to enter the trades the dead beneath their desks,

Modiano, Saltiel, Angel, once practiced here in Thessaloniki, though their bones
were turned over and over with bulldozers here in Thessaloniki, *Mother of Israel.*

A YELLOW HOUSE IN THESSALONIKI, 1943

You won't learn how the people vanished
by reading words on the train station plaque
mounted about two hundred meters
from the yellow house beside the tracks.

At a table men drink soda, smoke, laugh.
Only one wants to tell you the facts
of how the occupying Germans ran
the yellow house beside the tracks.

The grand villa was built so long ago
no railway ran through the flats.
Perfect for their purposes that chance
put the yellow house beside the tracks.

They rounded up the Jews at night. The station
wasn't used, allowing public distraction
when they packed families in the basement
of the yellow house beside the tracks.

Look at that boxcar painted lime green.
It is an Army office now for the lower ranks
says the sign on the door that opened
to the yellow house beside the tracks.

The head-high window is fitted with bars
and a small screen. You see leaves, blue sky in slats.
How could they breathe in there, those herded
from the yellow house beside the tracks?

Upstairs soldiers processed papers. Downstairs
below the planks, they heard the smack
of stamps, and agonized what was next
after the yellow house beside the tracks.

They loaded them into the livestock cars
labeled with the number of people. Backs
aching, they stood headed toward the camps
from the yellow house beside the tracks.

In April yellow daisies do not toil. They grow
in the field, heads spinning, when yellow sun acts
on them. One spring yellow stars were crowded below
in the yellow house beside the tracks.

DAY BREAKS ON ANDROS, 1944

When all at once dogs bark from the cobblestone
labyrinth in my nightmare and donkeys clop,
more burdened than ever, and the roosters panic
with church bells, footsteps, a screaming lamb,

I think, they know who I am, and they'll take me away…
at last, they've identified me, however narrowly.

Cerberus howls his unwanted welcome;
the doves grunt with the weary souls
in the underworld.

Then just as suddenly I wake, a taste on my tongue
like something spoiled. The red hibiscus flowering
outside the window spins a second among sunrays,
then stops. A gust of wind.

I'm on the island, safe for now.

I reach for my glasses on the nightstand,
put them on, and the room's colors shift into focus.
Then I turn my head slowly on the pillow,
almost afraid to reassure myself.

My daughter is asleep, there on the small bed
next to mine, her lips moving a little,
her braid coiled along her neck, her hand resting
on the chest of her doll.

I remember it is Easter Sunday and the scream
I heard was the lamb carried off to be slaughtered.
Today I will celebrate, too, posing as a Christian,
and I will call out with the rest, *Christos anesti*!
Christ has risen.

We've been passed over. I allow
sleep to lay its heavy body on mine
and I sink beneath it for a few more hours,
still and dreamless.

ISLAND ELEGY

The shopkeeper's canary warbles a few notes
and I sit up in my chair, waiting for his aria.
Through the transom window

the corner of the neighbor's house
is a blank piece of paper
held up against sky.

My ear wanders narrow passages
of the village labyrinth,
spiraling streets where at noon

between whitewashed walls
sun and blue sky come to a crescendo.
So much sunlight tricks me

into forgetting a moment the chill
that keeps me indoors, away from the sea.
The canary stops.

I listen in-between
chirps of sparrows who chatter about nothing
except the joy of being in a crowd, I guess.

I heard my friend's voice too briefly
and strain to hear him
again in the bright silences.

RED PICNIC, 1946

We spread our picnic on a red blanket on the beach
and our daughter plays in the shallows where Chagall's
paintbrush mixes ultramarine with sand.

You hold my hand and I feel my body rising
like a kite above us, above you and me
and our Eleftería's joyous white splash,

and the red tile roofs of the village grouped
across the hills that embrace the beach.
There are no eyes peering out from the eaves.

There are no houses turned upside down.
There's the carafe of burgundy on the red blanket
And just a little food. A tomato. An end of bread.

So much beauty, to name it feels almost like peace,
like sorrow to name it, too, as if my words
could save the picture of you smiling at us

or the wine warm in my throat, making my hip
curve upward just like your red grin, or my violet dress
fluttering against my skin like many wings,

or our daughter Eleftería in a ruby bathing suit,
her pale fingers waving from the sea,
the deep paint still shining blue and wet.

GREEK CIVIL WAR, 1949

Then after the Germans left, we Greeks fought
each other and the children were kidnapped to the Balkans
to learn to be good citizens. I saw the sun was too bright

and cut like a blade in the street where a man hobbled
on one leg and a cane. A stillness came from out of time

and stood radiating on the stone, as if the sun, in a brilliant helmet
and resting his bayonet on his shoulder, gloated, triumphant
to shine where a man's leg had been,
to warm the remaining foot in its boot, to heat the rivets
into two rows of absurd stars glowing on leather
while passersby carried home
bags of tomatoes, greens, and young zucchini.

Too many shoes, I thought.
They would be home before noon, I thought.

We Greeks know to wear a hat, to get out of the heat,
not to get sunstroke. Too often in the aftermath, when I opened
the shutters in the morning, angels crowded the sunlight.

I had to turn my face and close my eyes for a moment—
how could I help it? They were too bright and too thin,
striped cloth fluttering against the blue numbers on their skin.

Sometimes when I bent to put on my shoes, I'd find them
in uneasy sleep. There between the tongue and the laces,
there between the ground and the wire fences,
they were chilled and curled up, knees to chin,
among their crumpled wings, their translucent wings.
How could I put my shoes on then?

And was I crazy to walk barefoot to the sea?
"Where are your shoes?" the Greeks called out,
"Lady! Where are your shoes?"

Maybe I'm not a Greek. I lay down on the beach at noon
because I am a Jew and wanted to feel the hard sand
against my belly. The days the angels came I couldn't eat,
though I wouldn't starve as they did. I was empty
and the sun would make me sick. So I was stupid
listening to sea. Feeling the grit against my cheek,
the sand in my ear, I could hear muffled footsteps, orders, carts,
train wheels rolling toward me on waves marching in from the horizon.

The angels stood on my back and told me
the terrible things I didn't see.
But I can't remember them so well…the voices of the dead,
their shoes, and the sun too bright, too hot to remember.

The blacktop sleeps. It is the void roaming about
    cities, fields, and mountains beneath a woman's wings
    that only unfurl on moonless October nights,
    that are visible only to the ginger cat's eyes.
Sometimes when I'm alone I strike the motherlode, swinging my pick-ax
    at the past. There's no certainty any of us will live
    long enough to collect a pension. So few of the old

in skullcaps and headscarves survive the unsolved.
    How the palm fronds caught a thundercloud.
    Why all the food vanished
    from our children's bowls, even without a drought.
How the invading troops stole our heirlooms,
    why they snatched even our sheets.
    Why Rachel bled on the idols.

How Jacob made his pillow from the stone talisman
    of the moon-goddess, then dreamed
    the Lord's angels climbed down a ladder
    out of heaven and into his brain.
Why he anointed her remnants with oil.
    How to lose without hate.
    Why the mail arrives too late.

How to inscribe my face on the holy scrolls appropriated
    by the orthodox or will myself calm, smooth
    my collar when I am being lampooned.
    Why some could unfit themselves for work,
let themselves be called good-for-nothings. How some starved.
    Why some wrestle to be blessed,
    how some couldn't care less.

Now that I am feeble, now
    that I wrap my knees in bandages to walk downstairs
    and a sun-wrought filigree wrinkles the skin
    around my dark brown eyes, should I be aghast
that I hardly feel the shiver of adrenaline
    when I hear knocking at the door.
    Is it a shame that I've collected rocks

because they are pretty in my garden.
    For instance, the ore-stained sandstone contrasts
    against silver lavender leaves and the papery flowers
     of succulents called *little beauties*. They bloom in so many colors.
I've sorted through the heaps near the abandoned mines
    to calculate the density of history in veins
    of crystal amethyst, green copper, rusty iron, hint of gold.

I've lit lanterns and lain on my rooftop
    and watched how heavy hues spread across the village walls,
    how headlights steal across the panorama of roads,
    how the hairpin curves interlace hills and houses
and sparkling windows and streetlamps, all the way to the sea.
    Sometimes when I'm alone, my mind will exchange
    my memories for what I see in the present.

Gone for a moment are the black-booted soldiers
    whose helmets shadowed their eyes,
    who assembled in the marble squares,
    who stood on the jetty with their guns spearing the stars.
And now in the yellow glare of the harbor's mercury lights
    is stunning Ioanna, the port police officer
    in her spotless white uniform.

Her eyes are so dark, she need not line them with kohl.
    Her breasts are ample but her waist is not.
    She is mindless of admirers,
    for she averts the chaos of people loaded with baggage,
of motorbikes, cars, and trucks hauling goods.
    She directs the lines onto the night ferry
    without maybes, without a smile.

GOD'S CONFESSION

I am God and I am broken.
Every sunset I button the moons of my black robes

sequined with star, and in the morning
I choose a raiment of gray velvet cloud

or my sky blue silk, or else if I'm bored
I make a print of scattered showers,

partly sunny, and a rainbow here and there
to remind the humans of our covenant.

I want to look good, so they will love me.
Oh, yes, I want to be adored.

Am I noticed?
I might as well not exist.

I, God the Almighty, sigh aloud and give rise
to the wind kicking up, a hurricane--

and I break my promise again.
Oh, look, a city's gone. The poor people drowned

and left their hats to float a spell
on turbid waters, a memento of flesh

and breath, soon sucked under.
Gone are their dogs and kitty-cats,

roosters, hens, round sunny chicks, and the rats.
A lone canary still warbles from his cage

nailed to the eaves. That bird is no dove,
no olive branch in his beak.

He's just lucky his owners lived on high ground
and placed him higher. The orphans cry

for their parents, and the mothers and fathers
cry for their children. And down goes the ark.

I am that I am, I proclaim--can't they see
how lonely heaven is, as bored and broken, I watch

the mess I made on earth?
The planet spins before my ubiquitous eye,

torments me with the image of myself.
The toy soldiers are arrayed in line after line,

goose-stepping and saluting.
Their little uniforms are neat,

their guns and boots polished bright.
In the beginning

they are orderly.
Then they do their jobs:

plunder, torture, killing, and rape, blah, blah, blah, with prayers.
The usual. Damn them.

Listen, down there,
I am God the Father!

And I am bored by these dreadful words. Why bother
to inscribe them again on history.

I say unto them: *And when you spread out your hands,*
I will hide My eyes from you.

Even though though you make many prayers,
I will not hear.

Your hands are full of blood.
My hands are full of blood,

though I was to be the Prince of Peace.
Ah, how I would love a family.

The universe I created
with its orbits, explosions, and gasses,

continues in the clockwork of
my massive brain, and I roil in space,

in my own domain, my nothingness.
I am so lonely. No wonder

I change my shirts.
I want to seduce the world with my beauty.

If only she would come to me,
as if I were a boy whose play has gone terribly wrong.

If I could lie in her arms,
her eyes my mirror—and I could see her

smoothing the place where my great aching mind dwells,
comforting me and murmuring,

you are forgiven.

Dear God, Dear Dr. Heartbreak

CLEAN MONDAY

Dark ceases in his light, so they say.
I want to belong to him lifelong.
Same old song, old song, old song.

Black leaves in daylight.
Black leaves rot on the lawn.
Why have I done so much wrong?

Why do I see dark branches in blue sky,
lead filaments joining stained glass,
a cosmos that shows not the ark,

not radiant halos of the saints,
not his hand and kiss, his grace.
In my daylit trance the dark branches split

and split again, the patterns of my years
I should convert. I've been a bride
more than once, an unblessed fool

whose house is a mess. It is Clean Monday,
the first day of Lent, time to repent with joy,
as they do in Greece, to scour our rooms

of moth and rust, then go outside, uncorrupt,
and eat shellfish and octopus by the sea,
where clean-hearted souls fill the sky

with kites. If only he would invite me
to a picnic, too, and we'd eat Lenten food
beneath a plane tree ready for spring.

Maybe then I'd forget that same old song
gone wrong, oh Lord, and set aside my wit
that won't submit to trust or let me be adored.

And then it comes over me
     as the pianist hits
          the high notes
and the sax rises
     optimistically
          and the bass holds me with strength
onto the earth, so reassuring
     I can feel it in my gut and
          the drummer
closes his eyes
     and turns his face up toward
          the full moon he can't see,
letting the music of the rest enter him
     and somehow
          keeping them going by keeping time, of course.
And it comes over me
     that it's safe to believe,
          safe at last to love—
it comes to me
     when I look at him concentrated
          on the players, and he notices
my look and
     he winks
          and makes a quizzical gesture
with a tiny shake of his head that says,
     What is it?
          Tell me without a word.

A CHAT WITH GOD ABOUT THIS AND THAT

Dear God, today I'd like to chat about this and that
like pals, no thou shall and shall not, no calling up
to you from the abyss, no proving you exist.

Let's go casual, a blue jeans affair, and talk
about something dumb, a TV show maybe.
I don't watch much, don't like my eyes

helpless, drawn to the high rate of screen flicker
where crowds of incorporeal figures
speak new worlds into being.

I want to keep my brain waves clear
so I can receive you. Oh, God,
here we go again with the metaphysics.

Before we switch topics, I'm curious:
You're all-knowing, your attention omnipresent—
how many channels can you watch at once?

How many wars? How many lovers?
How many rivers flooding? How many wildflowers
blooming in how many climate zones?

Do you become numb, too?
Or can you resist being transfixed?
Oh, dear, let's get back on track,

have our chat about this and that.
Let's not mix up the ordinary
and the extraordinary. No kisses,

no flourishing, no miracles, no thunder,
no wrath, no death, no wonder, no one
wrecked like me. How about an errand?

Not the one into the wilderness—
I want the constant, the necessary,
say, grocery shopping. People commonly

advise don't go to the store hungry,
you'll buy too much. But I can't buy
anything unless my stomach calls me

to the tilapia, polenta, pistachios, parsley,
and oranges—then delicious Ls, Ohs, and Ahs
on my tongue prepare a Platonic ideal

of a meal to serve my loved ones.
Do I need temptation to nourish life?
Or do I need to need in order to create?

Or perhaps my divine concoction is made
with a little this, a little that. I won't name
the ingredients, the secrets of the trade

though you already know, having given me
all I am and all I possess and all I don't.
This and that are such boring words,

unattached as they are to earth or heaven,
unlike the earth and the heavens
in which you are manifest.

Or perhaps those words are free-flying birds
alighting on whatever they please.
Sometimes I'd like to stay in one place.

Give me some boredom, dear God, a balm
for my lament or praise or thanks to you
that nothing but nothing refuses to flower.

I'M JUST GONNA SIT OUT HERE FOR A WHILE

"I'm just gonna sit out here for a while,"
       he said from the balcony
              overlooking the port.
He'd smiled
       as he arranged an Aegean blue sarong
              across my hips, and I stayed on the bed,
listening,
       the night air whispering silkily on my bare back.
              Earlier Chet Baker sang my song,
"I fall in love too easily."
       I'd leaned my head way back and dizzily
              caught sight
of a shooting star streaking from 12 to 3 o'clock.
       With no moon
              and the mountains' edges and horizon erased,
the sea, sky, and land were one.
       A ferry sailed by suspended in black haze,
              and I marveled
how he made his voice go from so low,
       as if it came from rocks
              at the bottom of a pit,
and how with no guile,
       no obstacle,
              did he rise up in wonder.

Thank God for the family
    with the child too young
        to sit in the emergency row,
for the switcheroo
    that gave me extra leg room and a view
        of the jet's glowing wing, a mirror for his clouds.
Praise his many names for he shows himself
    to me as the Buddha in full lotus outside my window.
        Good to know he stays flexible, his endlessly
long beard blowing behind him,
    which looks like the jet stream
        to people on the ground.
Thanks for the company
    as I head for my new life,
        not the one in his paradise,
at least not yet, though I guess
    I'm passing through
        the heavenly home on my way.
Thanks most high I'm not unique and he wants me
    all for himself,
        even as no soul can belong to another.
Thanks for my jealous one and only,
    for my broken heart, for teaching my soul a lesson,
        the same old lesson of affliction taught us all—
only he completes me, right? I can't forget his face,
    can't forget what I can't have, can't
        let go or stop myself
from calling
    before boarding or crying in public
        as I lean against a concrete pillar,
murmuring I love you
    as if the words were holy, lonely, wholly lonely,
        and I alone belonged to him alone, leaving me alone.
And thank goodness the universe arranged
    to make me humble before the magnitude of love,
        that joke I sometimes get.

GOD'S GARAGE

I'm swearing, speeding through yellow lights changing red,
and the music on the radio breaks my heart—

accompanied as it is by autumn rain, the *kiss,*
kiss, kiss of windshield wipers, the harpsichord,

and the memory of your hands
on the piano or playing my ribs and hips.

I drive round and round the parking garage
praying for a space that waits just for me,

for something definitive
as the moment between the need to change

the light bulb that popped and turned black
and the moment I can see again,

the mundane task
and reading sentences.

I'm running out of time again, damn it,
and we were running out time

even when we were together.
With the gray expanse between us—

overcast outside, overcast inside—
I curse anything that may persuade me

there is grace: the radio infiltrating my small airspace
with a melody in G major that elevates the instrument's sorrow,

pulling it up, up from earth to ether—
maybe against its nature—and it resonates joy or faith.

Round and round I go, looking for a space,
chanting *it'll never work, never work,*

as if my psyche could be maneuvered.
I'd believe this truth: our connection is impossible.

I'd believe in truth and not *more impossible*
to stop wanting you and not *more impossibility exists.*

More likely that God is riding the radio waves,
attaching all things, particles and the peculiar,

damp cinderblock walls and the intractability of love,
mud-caked fenders and the sublime cello,

my litany of frustration and the synchronous playlist
that mocks me when at last I find a space,

as if to say, *You see how each gravitates inevitably to its place,*
and my relief revives the corny belief that we belong together.

And then my analogies don't match up.
I miss your smile after you'd parallel park with only centimeters to spare.

WHITE LEAVES AT NIGHT

I leave my bed, I leave my room
to go to the woods to look for him.

Above me branches shot with light
hold up a gossamer tent

where fans of white leaves
and stars block the dark.

No solace where I look. No moon
explains the trees' glowing bark.

I crawl on my knees on white leaves.
My clumsy white gown hinders my search.

White leaves make a bed where I cannot rest
nor lounge with him in a brilliant bower

nor find my way back to the shadowed room where he sleeps—
where he sleeps beside me but is not near.

First, curses when your love turns his back on you
        and curses when in turn you turn
        your back on him.
Second, as if the two were one and God were not
        beckoning you to come near,
        you turn your back on God, too.
Third, his words are a twister you hide from in the cellar
        and you won't fear him—I mean hear him—
        now you've locked yourself in the innermost room.
Fourth, you sit worthless on the earthen floor,
        and use your lucky penny to grind
        a tiny bit of mortar into sand.
Fifth, a sniff of still air evokes your question,
        Why don't schools here have windows?
        and the awful answer, *To keep kids from dreaming.*
Sixth, you're transfixed for the floor is a lake
        and your spirit is rowing across
        and your body wants to follow.
Seventh, your words leave things to chase sounds—
        if then for rhyme's sake you make amends,
        seven sins disperse in heaven's winds.
Eighth rhymes with faith in time's wake,
        and eight is the supine sign of eternity,
        standing upright.
Ninth, you petition the Divine
        for a prayer that is not
        comeuppance or vengeance—
Tenth, you start all over again.

WITH GOD IN THE MORNING

I can't go back to sleep,
so I weep, listening
for a rhyme.

For example, the morning dove sighs deep in my backyard.
She doesn't sing.
The Jehovah's witnesses rap at my door. They don't ring

my bell, in whose metal the word "peace" is cast.
How sweet are these witnesses, who stand at my threshold
and do not pass through, who honor you with formal dress,

expectant, smiling, their leaflets and Bibles held to their hearts.
They apologize for waking me,
though their mission is to wake me,

and leave me
with a little flier about why to read your word.
They promise to return, just as you did.

They know your name is Jehovah, but I wonder
if you are a supernova contained
in each letter of scripture

or are you my Casanova, wandering across the globe,
entering so many souls with your flesh and blood,
pouring your light into their mouths with a kiss.

I make coffee because I will not sleep.
How can it be that I am not unique?
How can it be that I am what I am

just like them, who know the answers so well?
And now—Holy Christ!—the phone rings as if to answer
my disbelief in answers.

National Geographic offers me a free satellite map,
a gift I can keep, if only I will give a chance
to a DVD of their highlights through the decades.

A map from space!
Could the charted world make me
a way to travel to you?

Would you take me
in your arms again and again
would we ascend to heavenly realms?

I tell the woman reading from her script
that I don't think I will accept her gift
and my ridiculous voice cracks

at the thought that I might have told your witnesses
the same, just as I beg now for forgiveness
and ask, please don't call again.

That's okay. You're okay, she says, blessing me in her way.
Have a good day.
And then, dear God, I hang up the phone.

STREET SCENE WITH A TEENAGE GIRL

She stops to tie her shoelace, as if in open terrain—
and not surrounded by a mass of swift strides,

no cardboard where a beggar sprawls, pulling her
button-less sweater closed around her neck,

no addresses and jobs indexed by the scuff and
polish of shoes, the qualities of cloths and leathers.

She stops with verve, not saying a word,
for a moment fully visible, her body hunched,

a cipher of resistance, defected from the procession.
She looks down at her feet, unashamed,

simply tying a bow, her chin pointing
to her heart and her head bent swan-like

into the wings of her jacket while passersby
veer around her, as if by her directive.

DOUBT, WITH BEAUTIFUL CLOUDS

I am here, my body
        floating on a small green lake.
                My daughter and her friend are here,
jumping from the newly painted red raft.
        Here are the girls' splashes holding
                millions of instances of sunlight,
most of which I can't see, falling from the sky
        and merging with reflections of trees
                that are here, too.

I see them dreaming (or perhaps
        they are the dream) of their solid selves—
                sycamore, locust, maple, pin oak, river birch—
differentiated and identified, rooted
        in the lawns banking the lake,
                green on green, summer-lighted
and here with me, as is my memory
        of spring—the fleshy petals of magnolias, dogwoods, tulip trees—
                a blossoming image

for each name I murmur,
        almost a prayer
                for you to be always
here with me,
        just as our body of water is
                the softest skin touching our skin.
There above me are beautiful clouds.
        They are luminous water,
                moving slowly,

and I try to track the way
        they make visible energetic lines
                of the seas, rivers, and lakes—
the ripples' whorl,
        the waves' curlicues,
                the currents' scrollwork,
the calligraphy of all that roils below me in the deep
        that grows colder and more obscure.
                More obscure.

Why, I wonder, do the words make me
        so lonely and the mere thought of the dark
                doubt your light? Not a scientist
with almost no knowledge of the way
        the force of wind, heat, and cold act on water,
                it's unlikely I've got the physics right.
Perhaps the gaseous does not reveal the design
        of the liquid, nor the material translate
                into the spirit.

Nor is it logical to believe
        the *logos* makes the world, every cell
                charged with your love,
and you are here
        in all things risen
                from the dirt and cool mud
at the bottom of the planet's waters.
        And I guess you are in the clouds
                and in their reflections.

They say your pure body is seated up there in the blue,
        but I feel you untrue, far from me,
                when I look to your face,
your skin unwrinkled as wax
        forever. I'll never see gray
                in your hair or beard.
Always will your blood and organs be healthy
        and your muscles robust enough
                to lift the stone away from the heaviest tomb.

Even if you are in the girls' bodies curled into cannonballs
        and in the spray all around them when they plunge
                and in their laughter
when they surface, even if you are here,
        love in my body
                floating under beautiful clouds mirrored and
fragmented on the water
        into thousands more beautiful clouds—
                when I want you whole,

your body is breaking
        for me to be here and doubt
                and drift on a small green lake, my little heaven.

NOTES

Epigraph: Translated by Willis Barnstone, from his *The Restored New Testament: A New Translation*.

WILD WITH IT:
Rainy Ghazal: "Rain down rain down rain down rain down" is taken from a concrete poem by Mary Ellen Solt.

Walking Around Santa Cruz: The title and some lines are influenced from Pablo Neruda's poem, "Walking Around."

BLUE EARTH:
Greek Easter:
> *Kalo Pascha* Happy Easter.
> *Koritsáki mou* My little girl (literally my little daughter), a common term of endearment.

The Ferry to Serifos: Serifos is an island in the Cyclades in Greece.

Counting Time on Kímolos
> *Mizithra* Goat cheese that is softer, less salty, sweeter than feta.
> *Souvlaki* Shish-ka-bob.
> *Paniyiri* Festival, from *paniyiris*, meaning all come together.
> Manos Hadzidakis A well-known Greek composer and songwriter.

Pleasure Attained Morbidly, Corruptingly:
> *Doxa to Theo* Glory to God.

Go to the Good and Return with the Good:
> *Kafenéion* Café.
> *Mezedes* Appetizers
> *Sigá, Sigá* Slowly, slowly

EVA'S VOICE:

Biographical Note on Eva Victoria Perera, Imaginary Poet: Eva Victoria Perera (1917–2001) was the daughter of a well-to-do jeweler and importer, Jacobo Angel, and a pianist, Sophia. Jacobo was a descendent of the Sephardic Jews who came to

Thessaloniki after 1492. He met Sophia in Vienna where she was studying piano. Jacobo traveled widely and was passionate about the arts and intellectual inquiry. An unconventional man, he rejected subservient roles for women and was attracted to Sophia's strong will, humor, and musical talent. Both parents were ambitious for Eva, their only child. With their encouragement, Eva began to write and paint when she was very young. She devoted herself to poetry and considered herself only an amateur painter. Yet she was greatly influenced by the visual arts; she felt a particular kinship to the iconography of Marc Chagall.

In 1927 the Angel family hired a governess for Eva, Hope Parker, a grand-niece of the fiery Transcendentalist preacher and reformer, Theodore Parker. Fascinated by ancient Greek culture, Hope had came to Greece on a spiritual quest and as a rebellion against her New England roots. While in Thessaloniki, Hope fell in love with a charismatic Rembetis, who abandoned her when she became pregnant. When the Angel family took her in, she had an infant daughter, Ariana. As a result, Eva was trained in classical Greek and European literature, and more unusually for a Greek, in American literature. Through her mother, she heard classical music; through Parker, the underground music of Rembetika. Eva was fluent in Greek, French, Ladino (old Spanish), and English.

In 1937, Eva married Isaak Perera, a piano student of her mother's. In 1939, their daughter, Eleftheria was born. Isaak became an architect, but he was a talented pianist. The young couple lived with Eva's parents after their marriage. Their home was filled with the music of Isaak and Sophia, until the family fled Thessaloniki.

When the Germans invaded Greece in 1942, Jacobo had the wherewithal to buy the immediate family false Christian identities. He took them all to the island of Andros, where they were taken in by Christian friends, the Haralambous family. Andros is a green island, full of gardens. Though all of Greece was pillaged of food by the Germans, and many starved to death, the families managed to grow and keep enough to stay alive and relatively healthy.

After the war, Eva's family returned to Thessaloniki. Nearly all their friends and relatives were dead; 50,000 Jews from the city known as "the Mother of Israel," perished in Auschwitz. Eva, Isaak, and Eleftheria found the ghosts too painful and they left Thessaloniki to settle in Athens, where Isaak established his practice. Eventually, they bought land on Andros, and built a home there; the island that had been their refuge during the war became their sanctuary from the city. Eva wrote poetry all her life, though like Cavafy she never printed her work for the public, only for her friends (who included some of Greece's greatest poets of the twentieth century, George Seferis and Yannis Ritsos). After Elefthería grew up, became an architect, and joined her father's practice, Eva spent most of her time on the island, though she traveled occasionally. She met and befriended Chagall in 1952, on his first visit to Greece. She spent her last years devoted to "growing an Eden" in her garden, where she loved to have outdoor dinner parties for her family and friends. She died among her fruit trees and flowers on August 15, 2001. In 2003, a volume of her collected poems was published in Greece, edited by her daughter, Elefthería, and her granddaughter, Sophia.

The Destruction of the Jewish Graveyard, Thessaloniki, 1942: In 1942 the Germans sent 7,000 Jewish men to work camps, in which the conditions were abysmal. Dr. Max Merton, the head of the German military administration demanded a ransom of 3.5 billion drachmas to release them, one billion of which would cancel the confiscation of the Jewish cemetery. The Jewish community refused to use the cemetery as an object of transaction but paid 2.5 billion in ransom to bring the men home. The agreement was signed and the men were released. But seven weeks later the two-thousand year old Jewish cemetery was confiscated, with the cooperation of Greek city officials, who for years had wanted to expand Aristotle University. New university buildings were built on the land that had held a half-million graves. Every piece of marble and brick was used as building material: the marble of the tombstones was used to repair churches damaged in the Italian air raids, as doorsteps of homes, to construct roads, and to build swimming pools for the Germans. The men's homecoming was a temporary reprieve. In 1943 they joined the 50,000 Jews from Thessaloniki who were deported to Auschwitz.

market song Greece won the first Allied Victory against the Axis. On October 28, 1940, the Greek Prime Minister, Ioannis Metaxas, rejected Mussolini's demand that Greece allow the Axis forces to enter Greece with one word, "ochi" or "no." The Italians invaded, and the Greeks forced their opponents to retreat and managed to occupy one quarter of Albania. Now October 28th is celebrated as Ochi Day throughout Greek communities and is a national holiday in Greece. In April the Germans invaded and defeated the Allied forces. The Germans requisitioned almost all foodstuffs and raw materials, which resulted in the Great Famine of 1941-42 and the deaths of 300, 000 Greeks, and perhaps more. German soldiers robbed the Greeks of their possession, and were even so bold as to hold women up in the streets and demand their jewelry.

Greek Civil War, 1949 During the Greek Civil War tens of thousands of Greek children were "evacuated" from the war front. Many of them were sent to the Eastern Block to be indoctrinated as communists.

God's Confession Quotation is Isaiah 1:15

Clean Monday Clean Monday or Bright Monday is the first day of Lent in Eastern Orthodoxy and is a national holiday in Greece. People clean their homes, fly kites, and go on outdoor excursions. Shellfish and octopus are Lenten foods.